LESS THAN ONE PERCENT

IMAMU TOMLINSON, MD, MBA

<1%

LESS THAN ONE PERCENT

HOW DISRUPTORS *DEFY THE ODDS*

Forbes | Books

Copyright © 2025 by Imamu Tomlinson, MD, MBA.

All rights reserved. No part of this book may be used or reproduced in any manner whatsoever without prior written consent of the author, except as provided by the United States of America copyright law.

Published by Forbes Books, Charleston, South Carolina.
An imprint of Advantage Media Group.

Forbes Books is a registered trademark, and the Forbes Books colophon is a trademark of Forbes Media, LLC.

Printed in the United States of America.

10 9 8 7 6 5 4 3 2 1

ISBN: 979-8-88750-602-9 (Hardcover)
ISBN: 979-8-88750-603-6 (eBook)

Library of Congress Control Number: 2024916060

Cover design by Megan Elger.
Layout design by Ruthie Wood.

This custom publication is intended to provide accurate information and the opinions of the author in regard to the subject matter covered. It is sold with the understanding that the publisher, Forbes Books, is not engaged in rendering legal, financial, or professional services of any kind. If legal advice or other expert assistance is required, the reader is advised to seek the services of a competent professional.

Since 1917, Forbes has remained steadfast in its mission to serve as the defining voice of entrepreneurial capitalism. Forbes Books, launched in 2016 through a partnership with Advantage Media, furthers that aim by helping business and thought leaders bring their stories, passion, and knowledge to the forefront in custom books. Opinions expressed by Forbes Books authors are their own. To be considered for publication, please visit **books.Forbes.com**.

To Michael Tomlinson and Pauline Tomlinson

What we say isn't always what we mean. What we mean isn't always what we feel. What we feel isn't always what we say …

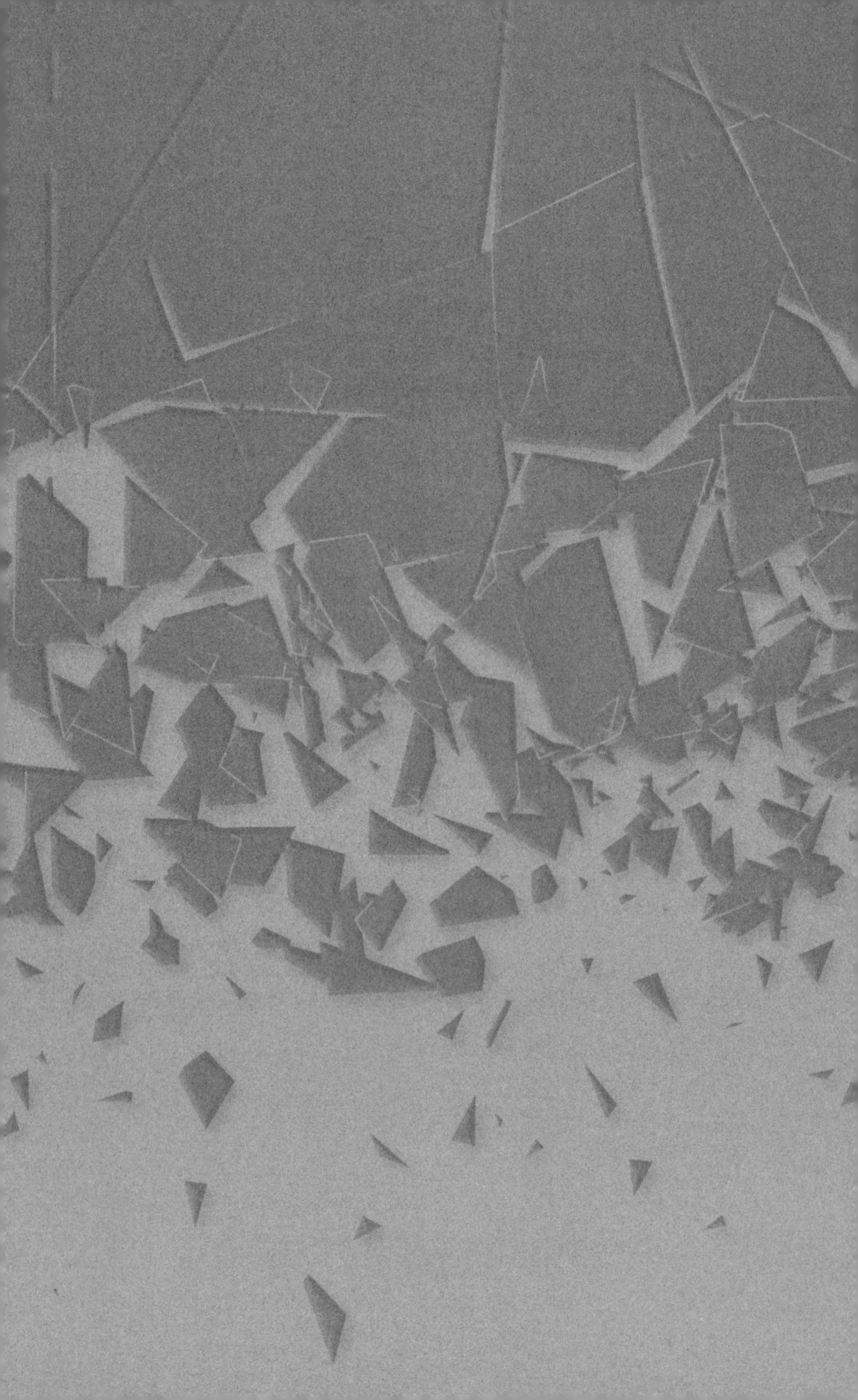

CONTENTS

ACKNOWLEDGMENTS............................IX

FOREWORD....................................XI
By Earvin "Magic" Johnson

CHAPTER 1......................................1
<1 Percent

CHAPTER 2......................................5
256th

CHAPTER 3....................................11
Bob McKillop, Corey Claitt, and Byron Faison

CHAPTER 4....................................17
Undefeated

CHAPTER 5....................................21
We Have a Problem

CHAPTER 6.. 27
Waiting Room

CHAPTER 7.. 33
Poison Ivy

CHAPTER 8.. 43
Fallacies

CHAPTER 9.. 55
Barry O'Shea

CHAPTER 10... 63
Wi Likkle But Wi Tallawah

CHAPTER 11... 75
Majority Rules Rule

CHAPTER 12... 87
Insolence

CHAPTER 13.. 101
To Morrow's Last Chance

CHAPTER 14.. 115
Disruptors

CHAPTER 15 .... **133**
Scary Giraffe

CHAPTER 16 .... **139**
Nanny

CHAPTER 17 .... **147**
An Apple a Day

CHAPTER 18 .... **159**
Them Want to See the Truth

CHAPTER 19 .... **169**
Nassau and Macao

CHAPTER 20 .... **183**
Deception

CHAPTER 21 .... **191**
Consciousness

CHAPTER 22 .... **201**
Boxes

DENOUEMENT **209**
Spiritual Leader

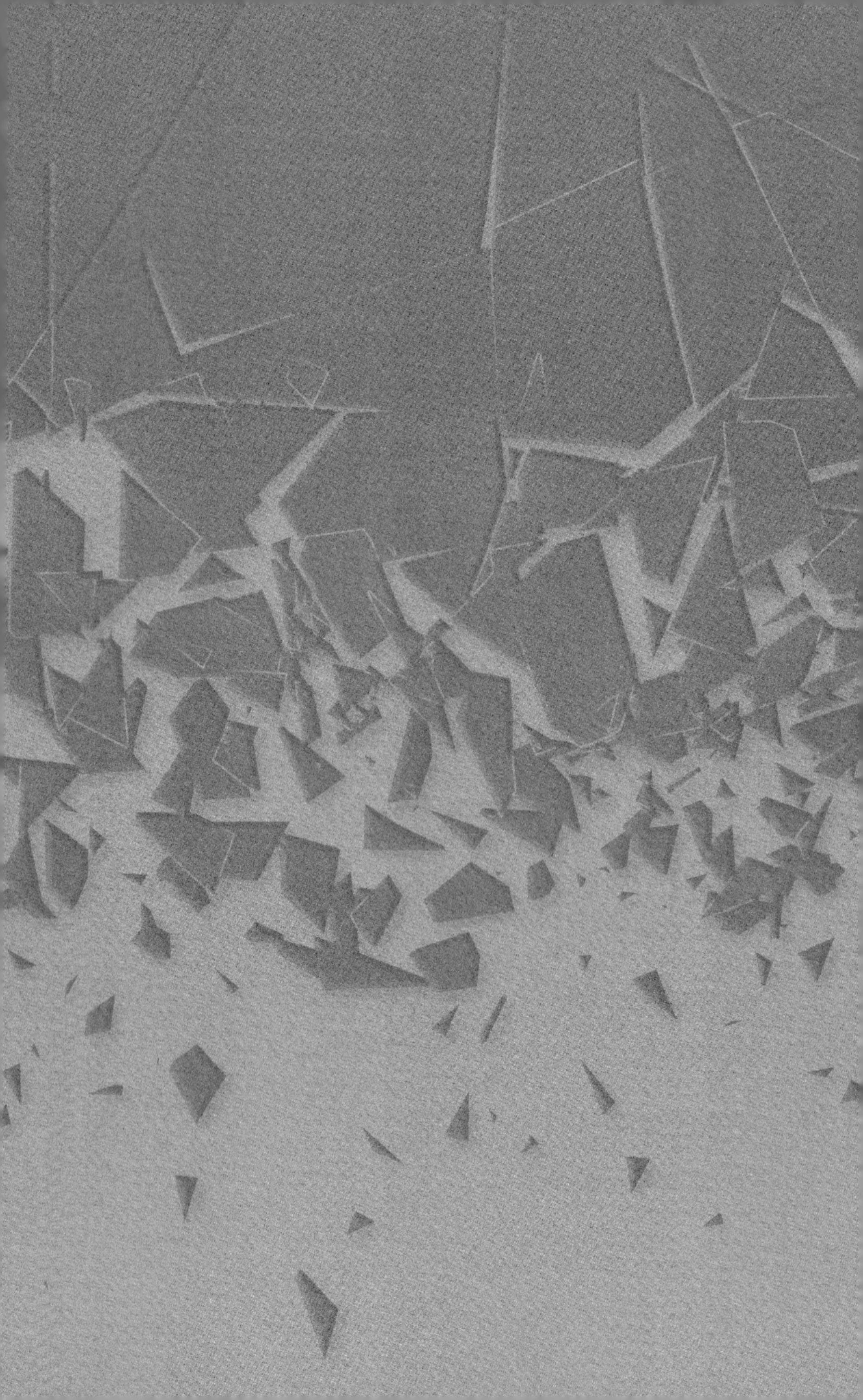

ACKNOWLEDGMENTS

There are so many who have helped make this project possible. It would be impossible to list all of you, but I hope you know I couldn't have done this without you.

I'll start by thanking Magic Johnson and his inspiration to follow through and complete this work. Specifically, he told me, "This story needs to be told!" Those words resonated with me so profoundly and became the major reason I felt I had to share this view of the world.

I would like to thank Vituity for giving me the opportunity to lead such a wonderful organization that is focused on improving as many lives as humanly possible.

I'd like to thank Simon Sinek, who prodded me to find my "why sentence": to inspire others to do the work necessary to be greater than anyone thought they could be.

I'd like to thank my family and friends for tolerating my philosophical banter and allowing me to share some of their stories in this book.

I'd like to thank my parents, who instilled in me the stubborn confidence necessary to try to change the things that others said I couldn't—and also for their part as biased reviewers and editors.

I'd like to thank Forbes Books for believing in me as a writer who happens to be a CEO, rather than a CEO who writes.

Most of all I am thankful to you for taking the chance to see a slightly different world—a world where everyone has a chance to make their mark, no matter who they are or where they are from.

Thank you for diving into the world of the less than one percent!

FOREWORD

BY EARVIN "MAGIC" JOHNSON

In the world of sports, I've seen many people exceed expectations, redefine norms, and overcome odds. I've seen underdogs rise to the occasion, proving that standards can be shattered and that limitations are often only illusions.

Even though I was the first pick in the 1979 National Basketball Association (NBA) draft, many people told me I couldn't be a six-foot-nine point guard. I didn't fit the mold. But for me, that didn't matter. I wanted to put my stamp on the NBA at the point guard position. That is the same approach I have used in my life beyond basketball. Whether it's on the court, in the classroom, or in the board room, I believe we should always challenge society's predetermined norms and push ourselves to positively impact the world.

My friend and colleague, Imamu Tomlinson, has also put his unique stamp on the world. Over the years we have worked together to care for those who have been ignored by the system—a system that wasn't built with them in mind. In *Less than One Percent,* Tomlinson explores a world of contradictions and introduces us to those who have risked disrupting that world.

In a society overwhelmingly dependent on structure, standards are often used to determine who is worthy enough to succeed. But as Tomlinson provocatively asks, who creates these standards? More importantly, what happens to those who struggle to fit into those predefined boxes?

In *Less than One Percent*, through both heartwarming and gut-wrenching stories, Tomlinson elaborates on society's contradictions and how many embrace disruption to pursue greatness. Tomlinson challenges us to reexamine the structures by which we evaluate individuals and highlights the fortitude one needs to disagree with the status quo to change the world for the better.

In a world where conformity and predictability often take center stage, *Less than One Percent* challenges us to embrace the nonstandard, break free from the chains of convention, and dare to achieve the extraordinary. It offers a powerful reminder that greatness isn't reserved for those who follow the beaten path. Greatness is for those brave enough to choose an unconventional path.

Enjoy the ride!

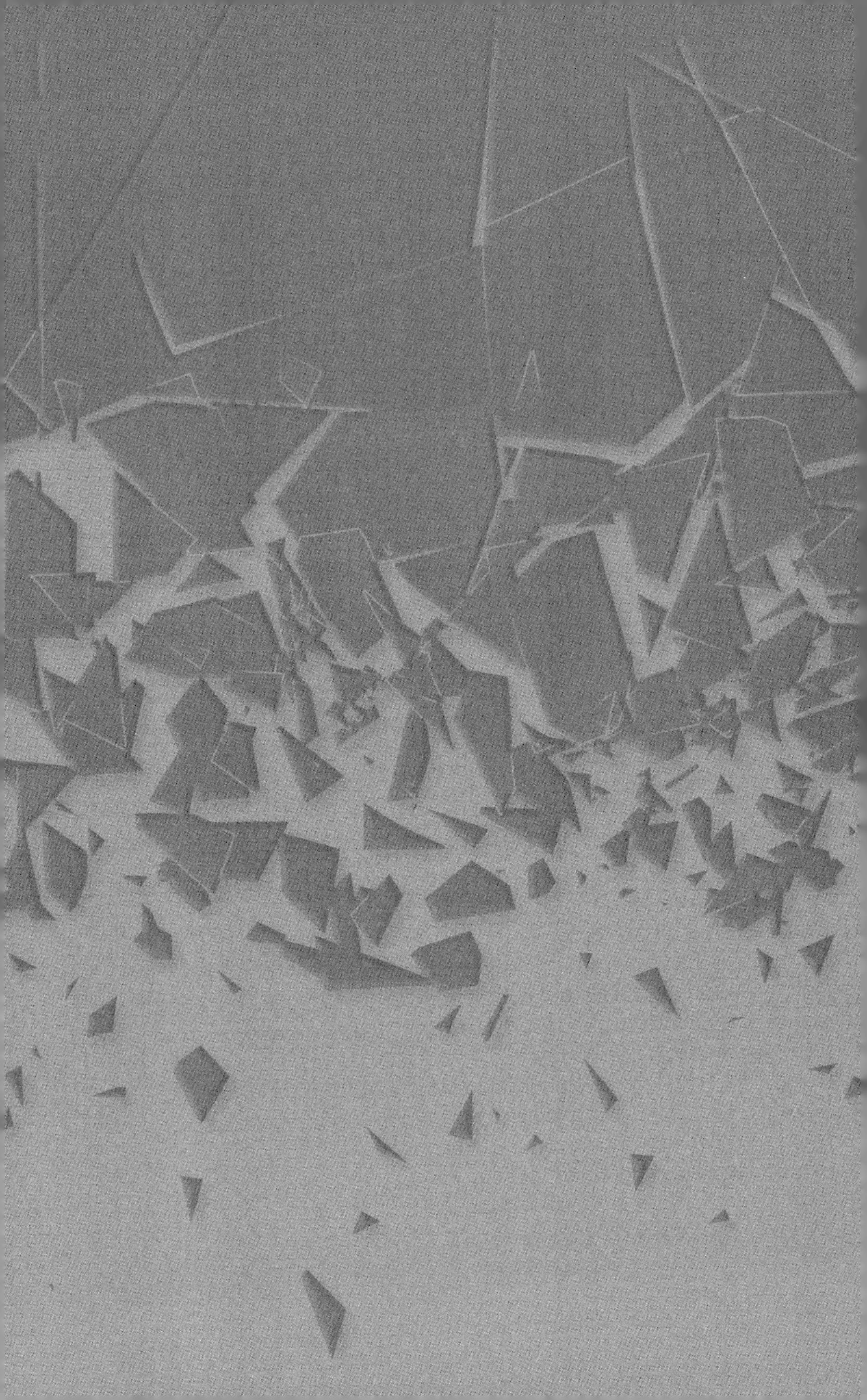

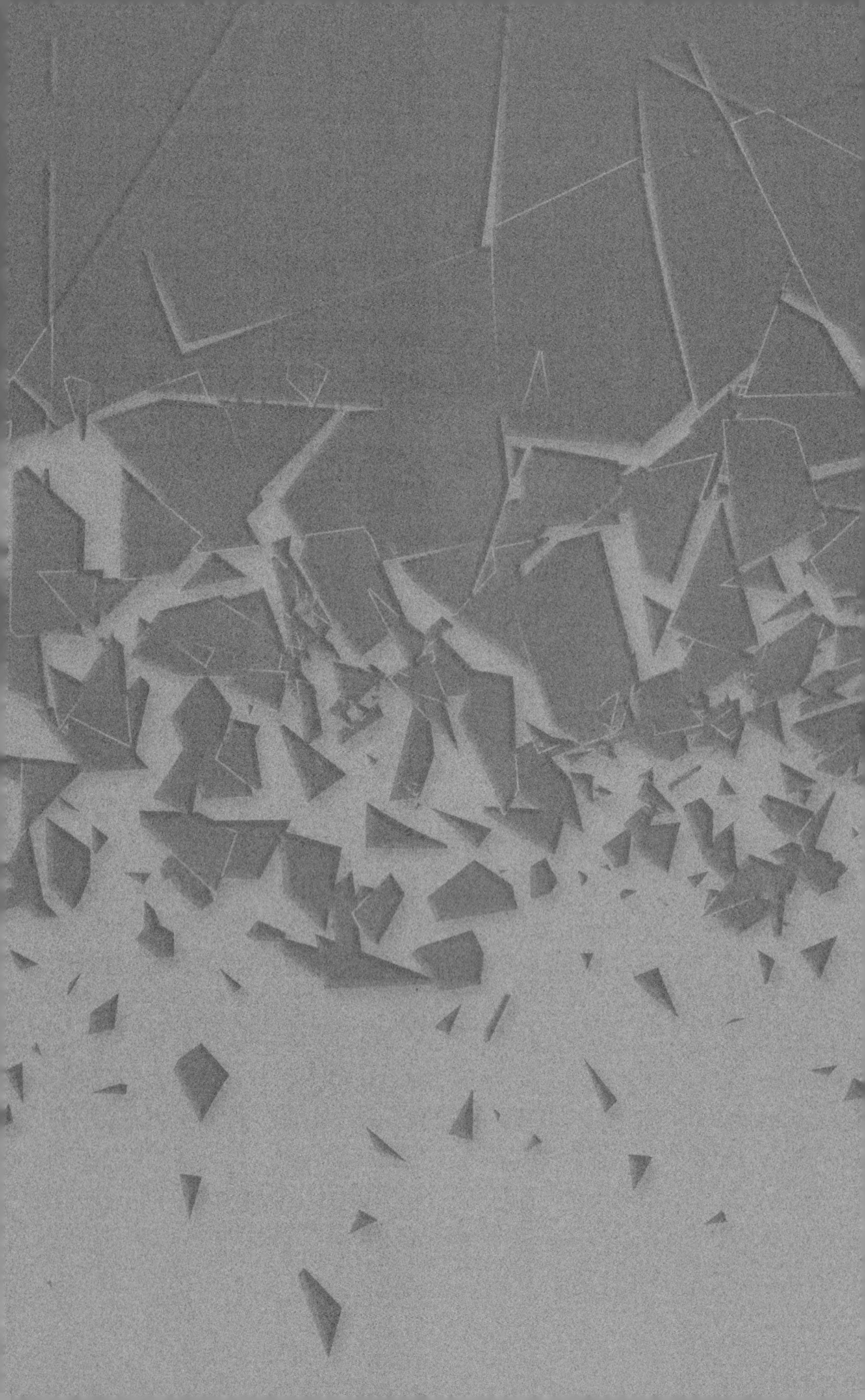

CHAPTER 1

<1 Percent

It is likely that unlikely things should happen.

–Aristotle

It was a typical summer day in 2016—the type of day when families frantically spend their precious time attempting to create memories. Parents think it's for the kids, but it's mainly for the future moments when everyone will regrettably wonder where all the time went. Even when everyone is giddy with the preoccupation of uninterrupted and overly orchestrated fun, there's always that one parent—the one inevitably preoccupied with the nimble task of multitasking. Fortunately, wireless earphones and the mute button can transform a monotonous and noisy car ride into an otherwise functional mobile office.

Participating in a highway-careening conference call is one thing, but this call was even more painful than that. As he compelled his spouse to pull over to decrease the risk of reception loss, he listened not so intently. Struggling with his propensity to say yes and his commitment to never let work become a career, he listened skeptically to career advice from his assigned coach.

He never really wanted coaching, much less career coaching, but that's what everyone does. It's easier to comply and not stand out. It was a trade-off. *Just agree,* he thought as he checked the time on his phone—again. After four long hours of driving, he was hoping to get to the beach before sunset. The best way to get off this call was just to be agreeable. Unfortunately, Disagreeable was his middle name.

On the other end of the call was a corporate coach—an individual charged with bringing out the best in people, subduing the worst, and finding the balance between the two. You know the kind! The type of coach the company puts in the middle of *he said, she said* to get them to *we said*—hopefully before they kill each other. Fortunately, it was almost time to start the summer fun. But then the coach asked him that question. The giggling in the background made it difficult to hear.

The coach repeated, "If you could have any job in the company, what would it be?"

The usually know-it-all middle manager was stumped while silently beckoning the kids to be quiet. After all, a job was just a job. If it were fun, it wouldn't be called work. A job was something you didn't want to do, so you could do the things you wanted to do—like the things this call prevented him from doing. His coach's question hit a nerve. He had never really thought about it, and now he was forced to think about it. After all, he was more of a just-send-the-check kind of guy.

Eager to wrap up the call, he brainstormed out loud. He told the coach he was particularly fond of numbers but wasn't sure he liked the idea of being a CFO. He liked detail, but the COO job seemed too much of a grind. He enjoyed selling but didn't like all the fleeting relationships that came with the territory.

He was always a team player, so why not lead the team? Confused but confident, he landed on a theoretical position. He said, "Well, maybe I could be the CEO?!"

The coach, recalling his client's anticareer laments, couldn't believe what he heard. The coach asked, "Do you really believe that? I'm not sure that could ever happen." The coach may have been talking tactically or politically, but it didn't matter. The pot was officially stirred.

Confused and slightly annoyed at the thought he "couldn't," he asked his coach, "What do you think my chances are?"

After running through the list of candidates, most of whom were more qualified and some better suited for the position, the coach answered, "Less than one percent!"

That reluctant, always-say-yes, career-avoidant middle manager was … me. And a few months after my coach's coaching, I became the CEO of a multibillion-dollar company!

My coach wasn't a bad coach. He was actually very insightful. He had counseled, assessed, and advised hundreds of executives. He wasn't wrong, and at the same time, he *was* wrong. We could probably stop there and chalk his error up to an utterly innocent miscalculation. But we can't stop there.

That seemingly innocent paradox is a miscalculation that is all too common in our society. From corporate America to middle school math to high school basketball prospects, we live in a society rife with similar assessment errors. We use our standard and conventional logic to confidently answer questions, even before we fully understand the questions we're asking. We create boxes based on what we think we know, without understanding that we don't really know much at all.

LESS THAN ONE PERCENT

It seems to work 99 percent of the time. But if we look closer, we'll see we're missing out. For an innocent miscalculated CEO prediction, there isn't much consequence for being wrong. In other matters such a prediction can inadvertently change the course of an entire generation.

My paradoxical CEO origin story isn't as rare as one would think. My seemingly unlikely career is the reason we should scrutinize society's compulsion with miscalculated assessments and closely examine those who dare to disrupt those assessments in the search of truth. This is a journey into the less than one percent.

CHAPTER 2

256TH

A paradox is a seeming contradiction, always demanding a change on the side of the observer. If we look at almost all things honestly we see everything has a character of paradox to it. Everything, including ourselves.

–Richard Rohr

Our society is obsessed with measures and standards. This awkward obsession gives us permission to be confident in our assessments. And that confidence is responsible for our nagging compulsion to determine who will succeed or fail—long before they succeed or fail. And why not? Predictions preserve our sanity. They provide stability and maintain our understanding of how the world should work. They provide order to our everyday chaos. What's more, our ability to predict allows us to allocate what we assume are limited resources to those whom we believe deserve them.

For example, the SAT—the test used to predict a high school student's future academic performance—is often used as a predictor of college success. Fifth-grade students who excel in math are placed in an enrichment program, while the underperformers are often left behind—even though they were *already* behind.

These are the social constructs we've come to accept and even rely on. These constructs create standards, and those standards reassure us. The world seems right when it follows predictable patterns. Those stabilizing patterns seemingly prevent the world from falling into chaos. But if we look at almost all things honestly, we may see that what we believe is predictable isn't always as predictable as we think. Our addiction to structure often unwittingly replaces truth with consistency.

Sentiment, opinion, and misappropriated logic guide our predictions. But looking at data might be more insightful. And a good place to find data is by starting our analysis in the world of sports. The best part of studying athletic contests is that they almost always have winners and losers. And because it's a billion-dollar industry, it's become big business to predict this big business.

To that end, sports experts and enthusiasts often try to identify the next big star. The sooner one can predict an individual's ability to succeed, the more relevant they become. The search for the best player has evolved into the search for the best *potential* player. Skip Bayless, Shannon Sharpe, Stephen A. Smith, and countless other sports analysts have built lucrative careers on analysis, consensus, and prediction.

People want to be right, and that rightness isn't necessarily about self-interest. They simply want to be a part of potential greatness. If one can't be the next big thing, then the next best thing is to be the

CHAPTER 2

one to find the next big thing. The basketball world is no different. Thousands of coaches, scouts, and writers spend hundreds of hours evaluating high school players to find the next big thing.

Much of a college coach's success rests on their ability to recruit. They must carefully evaluate skill, talent, and "fit" for their programs. But with thousands of players to assess nationally, coaches need help. Fortunately, they get that help from far too many analysts and evaluators who specialize in predicting that next big thing.

Height, weight, athleticism, and skill are tangible ways to compare basketball prospects. Height and weight can be directly evaluated. Athleticism can be assessed by measuring vertical leap, forty-yard dash, and bench press. Although not as straightforward, skill can theoretically be quantified by on-court metrics: points, assists, rebounds, and steals.

Writers and evaluators use all of this data to develop a consensus-based player ranking system. These rankings affect everything from college coaches' financial incentives to Olympic team selections. One would assume that a data-driven, logic-ridden, algorithmic approach would produce dependable and accurate results. If rankings were based solely on this objective data, their outcomes would be straightforward. Unfortunately, human beings are anything but straightforward.

If you talk with most evaluators and scouts, they'll describe something else they also use called "upside." Unlike the more objective and concrete data, upside is used to subjectively describe potential—a ceiling a given recruit can obtain. It's something intangible that people can't see that heightens the tangible attributes they can see.

Every year companies such as Rivals (a media outlet dedicated to college sports recruiting) and ESPN (the top sports network in the world) rank the top prospects in the country. They use a mix of writers and evaluators who have directly or indirectly assessed the athletes.

LESS THAN ONE PERCENT

ESPN typically ranks 150 of the best basketball players in the world. By far, it's the most prestigious list of potential future stars. ESPN's list guides the careers of all of the athletes on it. Unfortunately, that list also guides the careers of all the athletes who *aren't* on it.

Highly ranked players are sought after by the best schools, and many of those programs are often swayed by consensus. If ESPN says a prospect is number one, coaches would be foolish not to recruit that player. With every published ranking, superstars are born, and other careers are ruined. While there is often fierce debate about the difference between number ten and number twenty, there is typically widespread consensus that the first player on the list is a better prospect than the last.

Here are the top twenty-five male high school players from the 2006 Rivals basketball recruit rankings: Greg Oden, Kevin Durant, Brandan Wright, Spencer Hawes, Thaddeus Young, Chase Budinger, Ty Lawson, Henry Walker, Wayne Ellington, Brook Lopez, Javaris Crittenton, Paul Harris, Darrell Arthur, Daequan Cook, Gerald Henderson, Sherron Collins, Damion James, Stanley Robinson, DaJuan Summers, Obi Muonelo, Earl Clark, Mike Conley, Robin Lopez, Derrick Caracter, and Duke Crews.

High school is a long way from professional basketball, but several of these players went on to play at the highest level. As they should, the top high schoolers on this list eventually became top NBA prospects.

Or did they?

Evaluators don't only create player rankings. They also publicly document their evaluations to support those rankings. Rankings and their associated player evaluations are not-so-subtle ways to create consensus. This is the basketball world's way of determining who the winners are and who the winners aren't.

CHAPTER 2

Let's look closer at some other recruits on the 2006 Rivals high school basketball prospect rankings. Most of the top-ranked players on that list received scholarship offers from the best college basketball programs in the country. Size, skill, and athleticism made selecting a player at the top of the list obvious. But what if we look at the middle of the list? Or better yet, let's look at the very bottom.

At number 256 stood the most obscure recruit of all, barely 6 foot 2 inches and 165 pounds. That particular 256th-ranked player only had scholarship offers to play basketball from a few small schools—none of which would ever be considered basketball powerhouses. And the associated player evaluation was even worse.

Here are some of the comments used to describe the 256th player from the 2006 Rivals high school basketball prospect evaluation: "Not a true point guard," "Out of control at times," "Poor shot selection," "Stuck between two positions," "Lack of ability to defend at the next level," "Average athleticism, average size, average wingspan," "Frail frame," "Relies too heavily on the outside shot," and the most damning comment of all, this recruit had "limited upside."

That uncomplimentary evaluation describes a prospect who was unlikely to have an impact on college basketball. But that's where the evaluators, coaches, and writers were wrong. That skinny, frail prospect with limited upside, who was too small, not athletic enough, and took too many bad shots, became one of the best point guards in the history of the NBA. That less-than-one-percenter is Wardell Stephen Curry II.

At Davidson, Stephen Curry became the all-time leading scorer. In 2009 he was the most prolific scorer in Division I basketball. He would go on to be the seventh pick in the NBA draft. He would make the All-Rookie First Team in 2010 and the NBA First Team four times. Stephen Curry was an NBA All-Star eight times and league MVP twice, once by unanimous vote in 2016. At the time of this publication, he's won four NBA championships. He is also the all-time leader in three-pointers made in the NBA. Steph Curry's 256th ranking was a paradox.

On the other end of the spectrum, the first player on the list is 7-foot, 240-pound Greg Oden. At the time he was arguably the most dominant player in high school and was the consensus number one prospect in America. Almost every college offered him a scholarship—a promise of free education in exchange for his athletic prowess. Oden, burdened by injuries and expectations, played only three seasons and never achieved the potential his ranking predicted.

How were ESPN, 247Sports, and every other analyst so wrong? How did they miss one of the top five NBA players of all time? He was right in front of them! After Stephen Curry's story was written, everyone jumped on the bandwagon. Ironically, those same pundits who gave him less than a one percent chance of greatness are now calling him one of the greatest of all time!

In a letter to kick off his "Underrated" basketball camps, Steph wrote, "I think that's one of the biggest things I've really come to understand about myself over the last 17 years: The way that 'underrated' might start off as just some feeling the world imposes on you. But if you figure out how to harness it? It can become a feeling that you impose on the world."[1]

Apparently, Steph Curry hasn't forgotten. He has repeatedly used that underrated moniker, not only as internal motivation but also to help others who are in the same predicament.

---

[1] Stephen Curry, "Underrated," *The Players' Tribune*, January 9, 2019, https://www.theplayerstribune.com/articles/stephen-curry-underrated.

CHAPTER 3

BOB McKILLOP, COREY CLAITT, AND BYRON FAISON

What we see changes what we know. What we know changes what we see.

–Jean Piaget

Steph Curry's story should make us pause. It should make us realize that we trust our predictive instincts far too much. But is this really so bad? So we overlooked Steph Curry. What's the harm in that? Steph's poor prospect prediction was just a prediction. Predictions, by definition, are bound to be periodically incorrect.

Our faulty predictions misread the 256th-ranked high school basketball prospect, and that's one thing. But the nagging question that follows is something worse. How many other Steph Currys have we missed? Basketball is incredible with Steph, but how amazing would basketball be if we had more players like him? This isn't to take away from his uniqueness. Steph does things in the game of basketball that have never been done before. But if the evaluators had been right, Stephen Curry would've never been drafted, and we would've never had a chance to see the things we had never seen before.

The error of misidentification only tells part of the story. The success paradox is far more convoluted. How did Steph manage to avoid basketball obscurity? Because of their data miscalculations, most scouts, writers, and college coaches didn't believe Wardell Stephen Curry would become Steph Curry. Fortunately for basketball fans, at least one person didn't fall into that paradox. That person was Bob McKillop, Davidson's head basketball coach.

In a January 2022 interview with GQ Sports, Coach McKillop discussed his first impression of Stephen Curry, and it wasn't exactly what you would expect.[2]

> He played in one of the auxiliary gyms, not the main gym.... And he was awful. He threw the ball into the stands, he dropped passes, he dribbled off his foot, he missed shots. But never once during that game did he blame an official, or point a finger at a teammate. He was always cheering from the bench, he looked into his coach's eyes, and he never flinched. That stuck with me.

No, I didn't make that up. What was the thing that stuck with one of the only coaches who saw Stephen Curry's potential brilliance? Coach McKillop didn't talk about Steph's skill or prowess or athleticism or upside. He spoke of details that the other writers and scouts

---

2   Hanif Abdurraqib, "The Second Coming of Stephen Curry," GQ Sports, January 10, 2022, https://www.gq.com/story/stephen-curry-february-cover-profile.

didn't. And if the other coaches could see what Coach McKillop saw, Steph Curry's recruitment would have been profoundly different.

Coach McKillop saw something in Steph that was different. Conventional means of ascertaining Steph's potential didn't reveal the future success story he would become. Of course, using an unconventional approach to identify success factors makes Coach McKillop a little bit of a success savant. If the story stopped there, we would have learned about a unique way to identify untapped potential. But of course, the story doesn't stop there. Let's listen to Stephen Curry describe Coach McKillop's impact on him in a May 17, 2019, interview with ESPN senior writer Tom Junod.[3]

> He gave me all the confidence in the world, in terms of what I could be—in terms of being a man, the balance of on-the-court and off-the-court expectations. He was an example of that every day, and we had no choice but to follow suit.... He told me when I was a freshman that I had license to shoot any shot I wanted, but I'd have to work for it. I'd have to put in the time and actually commit to learning on the job. Even when I failed early freshman year, he stayed in my ear because he saw my potential before I did.

Coach McKillop didn't just identify that the 256th prospect had potential; he was a key part of Steph's journey. He gave him "all the confidence in the world." Steph was one of the only freshmen in the country who "had license to shoot any shot" he wanted, with a caveat. He's going to "have to work for it" and "put in the time and

---

3   Tom Junod, "Inside the Relationship That Unleashed Steph Curry's Greatness," ESPN, May 17, 2019, https://www.espn.com/nba/story/_/id/26709944/inside-relationship-unleashed-steph-curry-greatness.

actually commit to learning on the job." And if that weren't enough to differentiate Steph's collegiate basketball experience, there was this: "Even when I failed early freshman year, he stayed in my ear because he saw my potential before I did."

Coach McKillop was so confident in Steph's potential that he gave him permission to fail. That kind of mentorship and support fueled the 256th recruit to become one of history's best seventy-five players in NBA history. And Steph didn't let him down. Time after time, he proved his coach right with repeated exceptional performances, including an improbable run in the NCAA tournament. The rest is history.

Steph is special! But we would never have found out how special he was without a coach who believed in him so profoundly that he let him do things almost no other prospect was allowed to do. Steph has made an extraordinary living by becoming proficient in shooting shots other players didn't dare attempt.

To have someone believe in you more than you believe in yourself is one of the most powerful motivators in the world. Basketball is in a better place because of Stephen Curry. He has literally changed the game. He has broken every basketball convention on his way to four NBA championships. He has and will continue to break basketball records on his terms. As the 256th prospect in the country, Wardell Stephen Curry's chance of becoming the player we've come to idolize was so rare—those odds were somewhere around less than one percent.

Maybe not as well known as the 256th high school prospect in the 2006 high school graduating class were the 255th prospect Corey Claitt and the 257th prospect Byron Faison. Other than family and friends, most people aren't likely to be familiar with these names. Byron and Corey lived on either side of Stephen Curry's ranking. As hard as it is to acknowledge the giant Steph Curry evaluation miss, what happened to Corey and Byron may be even worse.

In 2021 the *Athletic* compiled a list of the top seventy-five basketball players in the game's history.[4] Let's look at a few of those top players and compare their associated high school rankings.[5,6]

Player	NBA Top 75 Rank	High School Rank
Stephen Curry	15	256*
Russell Westbrook	46	140
Kevin Durant	13	2

For the three players from the 2006 prospect list who were selected to the top of the NBA ranks, no mathematical, scientific, or logical correlation exists between their NBA and high school rankings. This paradox continues to play out year after year and class after class. Stephen Curry's story tells us a lot about his grind and work ethic, but his story tells us even more about those who weren't Stephen Curry.

Who knows how many other players could have impacted the game if we supported them like Coach McKillop supported Stephen Curry? How many other players could have had similar development if they had Coach McKillop in their corner, if they were given all the

---

[4] The Athletic NBA Staff, "NBA 75: Top 75 NBA Players of All Time, from MJ and LeBron to Lenny Wilkens," *Athletic*, February 23, 2022, https://www.nytimes.com/athletic/3137873/2022/02/23/the-nba-75-the-top-75-nba-players-of-all-time-from-mj-and-lebron-to-lenny-wilkens/.

[5] "Russel Westbrook," 247Sports, accessed June 17, 2024, https://247sports.com/player/russell-westbrook-64862/high-school-113666/.

[6] "Kevin Durant," Rivals, accessed June 17, 2024, https://n.rivals.com/content/athletes/kevin-durant-5049?view=pv.

confidence in the world, or if they had the license to shoot any shot even if they had to work for it?

Think of what other players on the list could have achieved if only they had been supported through their early failures. And what could Byron Faison or Corey Claitt have become if someone saw their potential before they did? Steph Curry succeeded despite the misidentifications and miscalculations, but he was lucky enough to have Bob McKillop.

Basketball's predictive propensity made the same mistake as my professional coach. Even with all of basketball's analytics, they still got it wrong. They got it so wrong that they were consistently inconsistent. Steph Curry's 256 prospect ranking was actually an amalgamation of several different rankings; during Steph's high school career, he was ranked as low as 300,[7] as high as 147,[8] and almost every number in between. Several of the most reputable ranking services refused to even give a ranking at all.[9]

How can we get better at predicting? How can we get more data to make our collective predictions more accurate? And that's the challenge. Predicting *is* the problem.

---

[7] Jackson Thompson, "Steph Curry Says He Learned Valuable Lessons about Patience and Believing in Himself That Propelled Him to Success," Business Insider, April 15, 2021, https://www.businessinsider.com/stephen-curry-high-school-drove-him-to-greatness-2021-3.

[8] "Stephen Curry," 247Sports, accessed June 17, 2024, https://247sports.com/Player/Stephen-Curry-65374/high-school-114673/.

[9] "Stephen Curry," Rivals, accessed June 17, 2024, https://n.rivals.com/content/athletes/stephen-curry-16883?view=pv.

CHAPTER 4

UNDEFEATED

> There is no exception to the rule that every rule has an exception.
>
> –James Thurber

On February 3, 2008, the New England Patriots were having what could be considered the most magical season of all time. They were the first National Football League (NFL) team since the 1972 Miami Dolphins to have an undefeated 16–0 regular season. They were led by their future hall-of-famer Bill Belichick and one of the greatest quarterbacks of all time—Tom Brady.

Undefeated through the entire regular season and postseason, the Patriots were one win away from football immortality. A Super Bowl victory was simply a formality for the heavily favored Patriots. All that stood in the way was the lowly fifth-seeded New York Giants. Every data point, analysis, and simulation led to the same prediction—a landslide Super Bowl victory for the Patriots.

However, the disagreeable Giants' head coach, Tom Coughlin, wasn't going to go down without a fight. After nearly being fired following the 2006 season, Coach Coughlin rejuvenated his approach. Instead of the military-style rigidity that was his calling card for most of his career, he softened and allowed his veterans to lead. Instead of his stern and private resolve—which often alienated him from his players—he learned to open up, to be vulnerable and connect. That revitalized connection was most evident with his upstart quarterback, Eli Manning.[10]

Despite his dry humor and reputation as a better-than-average practical joker, Manning was quiet and businesslike on the field. Coughlin's steely resolve and Manning's quiet confidence forged a team that embodied grit and resilience. They were a good match. The duo, often dismissed, cultivated a strategy rooted in their unyielding belief that they could defy the odds. Or at the very least, they could disrupt Tom Brady. Cast as mere obstacles for the invincible Patriots, Coughlin and Manning devised a plan to target Brady's strength.

Historically, Brady had been successful by throwing short, quick passes that were difficult for opponents to cover. Brady had mastered the three-step drop—a move in which the quarterback takes three quick steps backward before rifling the ball to the receiver midstride. In fact, Brady released the ball in 2.09 seconds. At the time that was the fastest in NFL history.[11] Because most of the Patriots' opponents

---

10   Ian O'Connor, "How Tom Coughlin Changed His Ways and Won Over the Giants," ESPN, January 5, 2016, https://www.espn.com/nfl/story/_/id/14504114/how-tom-coughlin-changed-ways-won-new-york-giants-nfl.

11   Jared Dubin, "Tom Brady Is NFL's Quickest Draw and It's Paying Off for the 3-0 Patriots," CBS, September 28, 2015, https://www.cbssports.com/nfl/news/tom-brady-is-nfls-quickest-draw-and-its-paying-off-for-the-3-0-patriots/.

were scared to give up the long pass, they tended to struggle with Brady's quick and surgical passes.

The Giants chose a different tactic; they decided to defend these short passes and force Brady to make longer ones. They surmised that forcing the Patriots out of their comfort zone would challenge their undefeated bravado. After a back-and-forth battle, history was made. The Giants shocked the world and were crowned 2008 Super Bowl Champions.

By all predictive standards, measures, and conventional logic, the Patriots should have annihilated their New York rival. The Giants won "despite sound reasoning from acceptable premises lead[ing] to a conclusion that seems senseless, logically unacceptable, and self-contradictory." That's the *Oxford Reference's* definition of a paradox, and that definition aptly describes the Giants' less-than-one-percent "upset" win.

We all have very well-reasoned retrospective theories to explain why underdogs win. At our core the underdog story appeals to us. It's an odd and confusing contradiction. We collectively agree on who is favored to win while secretly rooting for the unfavored to overcome. We all consent to the rule created by community convention, but we also revel in the rule's exception. We want underdogs to win precisely because we don't believe they can. Yes, human beings are confusing. We support and endorse the very rule that we hope isn't true. We create a rule and then expect an exception.

The truth is that the methodology we use to create rules is flawed. The Giants may have been perceived to be the exception, but maybe they were the rule. Predictive analysis is based on data and theory, but outcomes are the only accurate measures. If we look closely at the Patriots paradox, we'll see that it really wasn't much of a paradox at all. The Patriots were twelve-point favorites, and we expected them to win. Because they were undefeated, we expected them to continue to be undefeated. That hubris is the reason our predictions often conflict with our outcomes. The twelve-point favorites lost by three.

Exceptions happen, and sometimes underdogs win. Even David beat Goliath. Like other underdog stories, the Giants' win could have been the result of a fantastic anomaly. But this is something different. The Patriots paradox would be another statistical anomaly if the story stopped there. Of course, the story didn't stop there.

In the 2012 Super Bowl, Tom Coughlin and Eli Manning found themselves back in the championship game. Who did they play? You guessed it. They played Tom Brady, Bill Belichick, and the once again favored Patriots. David was pitted against Goliath—again. The exception again challenged the rule. Ironically, that statistical anomaly from their first meeting was so rare that it occurred again in 2012.

The Giants once again decisively beat the Patriots. When the underdog wins twice in as many tries, what do we call that? We call that a paradox. And it's the trap that we fall into. We were so wrong about the outcome the first time around that we made the same mistake when the same set of variables recurred four years later. It's the same trap that ranked 255 high school athletes higher than Steph Curry and the same trap that tripped up my executive coach.

Eric Bowman, a writer for the internet sports magazine Bleacher Report, made his prediction just four days before the second edition of David and Goliath: "In the end, it will be Tom Brady who leads the Patriots on a game-winning drive to win his fourth Super Bowl."[12] And of course, that never happened.

---

[12] Eric Bowman, "Super Bowl 2012: Spread Info, Line, Odds and Predictions for Giants vs. Patriots," Bleacher Report, February 1, 2012, https://bleacherreport.com/articles/1048400-super-bowl-2012-spread-info-line-odds-and-predictions-for-giants-vs-patriots.

CHAPTER 5

We Have a Problem

Recognizing a problem doesn't always bring a solution, but until we recognize that problem, there can be no solution.

–James Baldwin

So what's the solution? How do we unravel these paradoxes? How do we ensure that the next Steph Curry or potential CEO isn't left abandoned in a paradoxical quagmire? Before we can answer those questions, we must develop the ability to recognize our paradox problem. That's easier said than done!

Paradoxes are hard to see because we exist within them. It's similar to trying to determine the shape of a cloud when you're flying through one. Without evidence to the contrary, we happily participate and, in some cases, perpetuate paradoxes. Whether we're evaluating potential CEOs, finding the next NBA superstar, or choosing a college for burgeoning adolescent scientists, we must recognize these paradoxes early on. If we don't, we'll continue to suffer the retrospective regret that accompanies missing out on those who may change the world.

By taking the time to understand what paradoxes have looked like, we may be able to recognize what paradoxes *will* look like. If we develop this ability, we can avoid their seductive trap and inadvertently incorrect calculations. Success is fickle. It tends to avoid us, especially when we look for it. In the case of paradoxes, success doesn't mean being 100 percent correct 100 percent of the time. Success simply means decreasing our chances of making the same kind of groupthink mistakes in the future.

The first step in recognizing a paradox is to identify a convention. Dictionary.com describes a convention as "general agreement or consent; accepted usage, especially as a standard of procedure." Notice that this definition doesn't describe what's true. Instead, it describes a collection of consensual agreements about what a group believes to be true. This subtle difference isn't so subtle. By consensus, Steph Curry was the 256th not-so-impressive basketball recruit in that nation. Scouts, coaches, and writers all collectively agreed to that flawed and egregious assessment, which history has obviously proved wrong.

Dictionary.com also describes a convention as an "accepted practice that has become removed from naturally occurring behavior." Fortunately for basketball fans, Coach McKillop didn't accept that convention. His sensibilities about successful player characteristics outweighed the groupthink in the industry. He didn't succumb to college basketball's accepted practices—the same practices that couldn't and didn't acknowledge or predict Stephen Curry's greatness. This isn't to say that Stephen Curry isn't special or that his particular combination of qualities isn't rare. But rare things can't be found if you don't know what you're looking for.

CHAPTER 5

Let's look at the definition of groupthink.[13]

> Groupthink is a psychological phenomenon that occurs within a group of people in which the desire for harmony or conformity in the group results in an irrational or dysfunctional decision-making outcome. Cohesiveness, or the desire for cohesiveness, in a group may produce a tendency among its members to agree at all costs. This causes the group to minimize conflict and reach a consensus decision without critical evaluation.

Digest that for a minute. A group of people who seek the truth avoid that truth because of their need for conformity. Instead of focusing on what is necessary to reach the correct answer, they focus on what is necessary for group cohesion. And maybe the most unforgivable of errors is that they reach a consensus decision without critical evaluation. How can we possibly trust evaluators who evaluate by making decisions without critical evaluation? And yes, that sentence was just as confusing to me as it was to you. But then again, so are paradoxes.

To take this a step further, the *Merriam-Webster Dictionary* describes groupthink as "a pattern of thought characterized by self-deception, forced manufacture of consent, and conformity to group values and ethics." In other words conformity requires individuals to forgo the self-analytics necessary to determine the actual merits of an outcome.

Here is an example. Let's line up a group of athletes and determine who's the fastest. That should be easy—watch them race. But that's not what Steph Curry's evaluators did. Instead of meritocratic comparison through competition, they did something curiously different. If we

---

13   Jeni McRay, *Leadership Glossary: Essential Terms for the 21st Century* (Santa Barbara: Mission Bell Media, 2015).

followed their methodology, we would pick winners before the race. It may look something like this: Runner #3 has the longest legs; therefore, that individual will be faster because of a longer stride. Runner #5 is shorter but more muscular. Runner #1 won a race two years ago, and runner #4 looks more intense and is fastidiously stretching.

Imagine predicting a runner's greatness by visual assessment rather than the results of a race. Think about how ridiculous that sounds. Imagine a field of sprinters standing at the starting line while evaluators looked them over and declared a winner. This example may seem outlandish, but our society does this all the time. How can we create consensus about a runner's ability to run without seeing them run? Likewise, without seeing people succeed, how can we create consensus about their ability to succeed? Evaluators created consensus about Steph Curry's career before he even had one.

Even when people suspect a paradox is lurking, they shy away from rejecting the convention. They don't want to stand out. They want to be agreeable. Many people argue that a current convention or practice should stay the same because they can't identify an alternative. That's the true definition of groupthink—to continue to think the way one always has because it's too hard or too much work to innovate a new way of thinking. That way of thinking stifles creativity and creates false narratives about the infinite number of alternative successful outcomes.

The only way to objectively and accurately predict winners in our theoretical one-hundred-meter race is to race. Instead of predicting winners before the race is run, let the athletes sort it out. We live in a society preoccupied with predicting race results even before we give the runners a chance to race. And that's the true travesty!

Groupthink isn't just theoretical. The 1986 *Challenger* disaster was a fatal real-world example of this psychological predisposition.

CHAPTER 5

The devastating disaster that took the lives of seven astronauts was caused by a faulty seal in the shuttle's rocket boosters. The "O-rings"—the elastic piece of equipment responsible for maintaining that seal—failed.

The Rogers Commission Report, the commission responsible for investigating the disaster, revealed that many of the engineers "had reservations about the O-ring." One engineer in particular—Roger Boisjoly—violently opposed the launch because of this concern. Specifically, he predicted "a catastrophe of the highest order" to his managers. He voiced his concern about the elastic seals between boosters and their response to cold weather. And it wasn't simply a muted opinion. Boisjoly said he "fought like hell to stop that launch.... We all knew if the seals failed the shuttle would blow up!"[14]

NASA's George Hardy told Boisjoly that he was "appalled by your recommendation." Lawrence Mulloy, another program manager, was so incensed he asked sarcastically, "When do you want me to launch—next April?"[15]

NASA's leadership agreed, at all costs, to go ahead with the launch—choosing to ignore Boisjoly and the other engineers. Unfortunately, Francis Scobee, Michael Smith, Ellison Onizuka, Judith Resnik, Ronald McNair, Gregory Jarvis, and S. Christa McAuliffe paid the ultimate cost of NASA's groupthink.[16]

Even when lives aren't at stake, it's incumbent upon us to identify groupthink conventions and violently oppose them. We must channel

---

14   Howard Berkes, "Remembering Roger Boisjoly: He Tried to Stop Shuttle Challenger Launch," NPR, February 6, 2012, https://www.npr.org/sections/thetwo-way/2012/02/06/146490064/remembering-roger-boisjoly-he-tried-to-stop-shuttle-challenger-launch.

15   Berkes, "Remembering Roger Boisjoly."

16   Amy Shira Teitel, "What Caused the Challenger Disaster?" History, updated April 15, 2024, http://www.history.com/news/how-the-challenger-disaster-changed-nasa.

our inner Coach McKillop and Roger Boisjoly when we identify these groupthink moments. We need to use our individual sensibilities to assess honestly and avoid the allure of adopting unfounded standards.

Don't get me wrong, flawed standards can occasionally be correct in predicting the future. The same standard that couldn't predict Steph Curry's greatness accurately predicted LeBron James's rise to basketball immortality. It isn't a great leap to predict that a six-foot-nine, überathletic, highly skilled, high-basketball-IQ prodigy would likely be successful. But the less predictable get left behind, underrecruited, underrepresented, or downright ignored.

The reason to do things differently isn't because of those who fall into the strata of surefire future success. The reason to do things differently is to find those who can change the world, even when most believe they can't. The reason to do things differently is to find the less than one percent and to fight like hell to destroy the groupthink that can potentially distract us from the truth.

CHAPTER 6

Waiting Room

To arrive at a contradiction is to confess an error in one's thinking; to maintain a contradiction is to abdicate one's mind and to evict oneself from the realm of reality.

–Ayn Rand

Throughout history, human beings have intentionally and unintentionally surrendered to conventions. It's one thing when conventions bias our predictions of a seemingly irrelevant one-hundred-meter dash. It's entirely another thing when a convention is created by an immoral consensus. At one sad time in American history, collective groupthink resulted in the unfortunate convention that African Americans didn't deserve the fundamental rights given to other Americans. And in another not-so-distant time, a convention denied women the right to vote.

Those conventions were obviously immoral and unethical. Why did America take so long to recognize these inequitable conventions? It took 131 years for women to receive the right to vote and even longer for African Americans to be treated equally under the law.

Unfortunately, that's the nature of conventions. They're invisible until their unsubstantiated illogic is questioned. Questioning them requires the individualism necessary to break consensus and rely on one's distinct sensibilities. Just because everyone agrees doesn't mean what they agreed upon is correct—especially when lives are on the line.

Just as society once accepted the egregious conventions denying basic rights to African Americans and women, we have similarly entrenched conventions in healthcare that go unquestioned until they cause harm. Healthcare relies on convention to bring standards to patient care. It's so dependent on standards that appropriate patient care is known as "the standard of care."

Effectively treating illnesses requires scientific rigor and structure. Treatments must pass rigorous scrutiny before acceptance as the standard of care. You might expect that healthcare, an industry built on science and logic, would be immune to contradicting paradoxes. Or so you would think. As you have likely recognized, any discipline with standards is almost always susceptible to paradox.

If you were unfortunate enough to require emergency medical services before the late 1990s, you likely waited hours in an emergency room to get treated. If your life wasn't in imminent jeopardy, waiting was the standard of care. Early on, the consensus in emergency care categorized patients based on their presumed severity of illness. The term "triage" originated from the French verb *trier*, which means to separate or sort. The Roman emperor Maximilian originally introduced this concept for soldiers wounded in battle, who were categorized and treated by the severity of their injuries.

CHAPTER 6

Over the years the triage concept has been further refined and standardized. During the First World War, wounded soldiers were put into three categories: those likely to live with or without treatment, those unlikely to live with or without treatment, and finally, those for whom treatment could increase the likelihood of a positive outcome.

While the categories aren't exactly the same in today's modern triage, the fundamentals remain the same. You read that correctly. The standard of care for emergency patients is the same standard used on the battlefield during a world war. While there are some similarities between caring for those wounded on a battlefield and those sick and injured in an emergency medical center, there are also profound differences.

Wikipedia describes triage as "a practice invoked when acute care cannot be provided for lack of resources. The process rations care towards those who are most in need of immediate care, and who benefit most from it." This is the way most emergency departments approached triage before the 1990s. If you weren't in need of urgent intervention, you were deemed less of a priority. This convention was so ingrained that many emergency departments were designed and built with oversize waiting rooms. Emergency care was less about the care and more about waiting.

There is no question that healthcare has its challenges, but the resources required for a battlefield should be very different from those needed for an emergency department. The consensus in the medical community was that triage—with its battlefield roots—was the best way to appropriately care for patients. Yet despite overwhelming evidence showing that delaying care was potentially harming patients, hospitals and physicians continued this practice. Triage worked well for the sickest patients whose symptoms were obvious, but it didn't work so well for the lion's share of the patients who presented to emergency departments.

Unfortunately, that's not the worst of it. The consequence of the triage process is that many of the sickest patients were marooned in this traditional triage quagmire. The triage standard was to have one individual or unit evaluate and ration care sequentially, even when that process created a bottleneck. This meant the sickest patients were evaluated one after another after another. Every moment spent waiting in an emergency department isn't just a delay in care; it can lead to worsening condition, potential suffering, or even loss of life.

The emergency medical community continued this triage groupthink until one disagreeable physician in Southern California decided to disrupt that previously unchallenged standard. Dr. Michael Berger recognized that emergency department care was a paradox, and he was compelled to disrupt that paradox. With the help of his medical group, he developed a concept called Rapid Medical Evaluation® (RME).

Dr. Berger's story wasn't just one of medical innovation—it was a battle against an entrenched system. He faced skepticism and resistance, yet he persevered, knowing that lives depended on it. Berger challenged the convention. His disagreeableness allowed him to reject the consensus.

RME changed the triage paradigm. Instead of evaluating patients sequentially, the new methodology allowed everyone to be assessed as quickly as possible. Instead of reserving resources for the sickest patients, Berger and his team allocated different resources for different levels of acuity. Essentially, they saw all the patients simultaneously. Lower-acuity patients had designated resources and were treated on separate pathways from the sickest patients.

Under the old model, lower- and higher-severity patients competed for resources. Patients were numbers in a queue, waiting their turn in a potentially fatal line. In the new model, each patient became a priority. Resources were allocated based on each patient's unique needs rather than their position in line. Even in the fastest rendition of traditional triage, Berger knew it still fell short. Healthcare had to confess the error in its thinking. And maintaining that contradiction would evict one's mind from the realm of the patient care reality.

Assuming that the world's most efficient individual patient triage lasts an unrealistic one minute, the second patient in line is seen in two minutes. The old system isn't all that bad with one, two, or even three patients. However, problems arise when we get to the sixtieth patient in line, who doesn't get evaluated for an hour or more!

Seeing all patients simultaneously and more efficiently wasn't the only outcome of disrupting this long-standing practice. Unexpectedly, by creating different pathways for patients of different severities, Berger's emergency department decreased the overall patient load. This meant they no longer had patients waiting in the waiting room. In many cases these spaces could be allocated for patient care rather than patient waiting.

Confessing one's error—a flawed intake system for the care of emergency patients—led to a more effective model. Instead of a care standard developed for the care of the sickest patients, this contradiction allowed Berger and his team to develop a new care standard for *all* patients. Instead of creating a patient flow based on the available resources, he changed the flow of resources based on the availability of patients—which flipped the paradigm.

Dr. Berger and his group didn't necessarily recognize that they were in the midst of a paradox. They did recognize that the conventional way of doing things wasn't delivering the results that they knew were possible. They had difficulty maintaining healthcare's consensus-driven contradiction. After confessing that error, they knew that things could be, or rather, had to be done differently.

How did the emergency medicine community respond, the same community responsible for creating consensus around an archaic model better suited for the battlefield? They responded by universally adopting it. Today, RME is the standard of care in emergency medicine. The good news is that this new convention is far better than the previous consensus-based standard. The bad news is that the new model is the new consensus-based standard of care that almost everybody in the industry has adopted.

Do you follow?

The broad adoption of RME shows us that no matter how ingrained a convention is, change is possible. However, this broad adoption also shows us that the new convention is ripe for further disruption. To avoid complacency, the healthcare industry must continue to disrupt the current care to improve the future care. Recognizing conventions is only a first step. Conventions that are improved through disruption often become conventions that need to be improved through disruption. The vacillation between convention and disruption is the prescription that is necessary to make the world a far better place.

CHAPTER 7

POISON IVY

The only thing that is more expensive than education is ignorance.

–Benjamin Franklin

Standards are relationships between variables that are based on predictable heuristics. Mathematics and science, because of their predictability, tend to create reliable standards. The idea that one plus one equals two is an irrefutable mathematical relationship. That equation is repeatable and replicable. But a group of individuals who collectively agree that one plus one equals three have created a convention—that line of thinking doesn't follow the math.

Thus, mathematical relationships appear to be a reasonable and predictable way to create standards for the world to follow. These repeatable methods and known consistent outcomes can theoretically become the measure by which something or someone is evaluated. Theoretically.

Creating standards for widgets, computers, or peaches isn't overly complicated. Creating standards for humans, however, is far more complex. Even if we could all somehow agree on the definition of success, identifying a standard success process is decidedly more difficult. When it comes to society's collective interpretation of success, most equations look more like one plus one equals three.

We do this every single day. We focus on what we believe rather than what is true, and that modus operandi is the unstable substrate in which we attempt to catalyze our success. We confuse generally accepted practices with repeatable and replicable standards. We believe what we believe mostly because others tell us to believe it. It isn't our fault. It's an honest mistake. It's what we do 99 percent of the time. And that's why this book is focused on what occurs less than one percent of the time.

Almost every industry has its standards, and those standards create litmus tests to separate winners and losers. Education isn't any different and is often used as a litmus test for success. The relationship between education and success is assumed to be linear. Money isn't everything. But if we measure success in terms of future earnings, the more education you get, the more future income you stand to gain.

This linear relationship between success and education is part of school counselors' and parents' refrain to students. Their mantra? Do well in high school, attend the best college you can, and success—in the form of income—will be inevitable. The pressure to attend the best school is endured by students and exacerbated by their parents' anxiety.

Counselors, parents, and employers value education because they believe that better-educated students will have more opportunities. It doesn't stop there. Many stratify education acquisition even further.

CHAPTER 7

They believe that a good education isn't as good as a great education, and a great education isn't as great as an education from the Ivy League.

Brown University, Columbia University, Cornell University, Dartmouth College, Harvard University, Princeton University, University of Pennsylvania, and Yale University comprise the most revered collection of colleges in the country. The Ivy League derived its name from the ritual planting of ivy, a practice that originated in the 1800s. The first known use of the "Ivy League" reference occurred in 1933 by sportswriter Stanley Woodward.[17] He described this elite class of schools and the ivy that connected them. Since then, the moniker stuck.

Most college athletic conferences in the country have their own unique and differentiating characteristics. The Southeastern Conference is known for its überathletic athletes, while the Big 12 is known for its gritty grind-it-out football contests. Then there's the Ivy League, whose collection of schools isn't aggregated based on the best athletes or facilities. The Ivy League schools are aggregated based on academic excellence, of which they are unequivocally the best.

The Ivy League is the only athletic conference with the Scripps National Spelling Bee champion among its top recruits. Being a member of the most prestigious academic league in the country isn't just an honor. Membership in this elite group comes with significant financial success. According to the Statista Research Department, US citizens with a professional degree earn a median household income of $154,333. Those with a bachelor's degree earn $105,552. High

---

17   "A History of Tradition," The Ivy League, accessed June 18, 2024, https://ivyleague.com/sports/2017/7/28/history-timeline-index.aspx.

school graduates earn $50,401, and those with less than a ninth-grade education earn $28,294.[18]

While unquestionably valuable, that vaunted Ivy League education comes at a hefty price. For the 2022–2023 academic year, Ivy League tuition cost students and their overly supportive parents an average of $83,593. A nominal investment of $340,000 for a four-year degree can yield career opportunities far superior to their non–Ivy League counterparts. If you or your child progeny are fortunate enough to attend Columbia at $82,584,[19] Harvard at $84,413,[20] Dartmouth at $83,349,[21] Yale at $84,525,[22] University of Pennsylvania at $86,844,[23] Cornell at $83,296,[24] or Princeton at a mere $79,540,[25] you are virtually guaranteed success. Or so you would think.

All things being equal, future earnings appear to be proportionally tied to the level of education. Simply put, the more educated you

---

18   "Median Household Income in the United States in 2022," Statista, April 3, 2024, https://www.statista.com/statistics/233301/median-household-income-in-the-united-states-by-education/.

19   "Fees, Expenses, and Financial Aid," *Columbia College Bulletin: 2021–2022*, March 30, 2022, https://www.college.columbia.edu/sites/default/files/columbia_college_2021-2022_bulletin_no_course_listings.pdf.

20   "How Aid Works: Cost of Attendance: 2023–2024," Harvard College: Griffin Financial Aid Office, accessed June 18, 2024, https://college.harvard.edu/financial-aid/how-aid-works.

21   "Ivy League Tuition and Fees 2022–23," College Essay Advisors, accessed June 18, 2024, https://www.collegeessayadvisors.com/ivy-league-tuition-and-fees-2022-23/.

22   "Socioeconomic Diversity," *Diversity at Yale College, 2022–2023*, October 21, 2022, https://bulletin.yale.edu/sites/default/files/diversity-2022-2023.pdf.

23   College Essay Advisors, "Ivy League Tuition and Fees 2022–23."

24   College Essay Advisors, "Ivy League Tuition and Fees 2022–23."

25   Julie Bonette, "Princeton Will Be Free for Families Earning under $100,000," *Princeton Alumni Weekly*, October 2022, https://paw.princeton.edu/article/princeton-will-be-free-families-earning-under-100000.

are, the more money you earn.[26] However, the relationship between education and greatness is far from linear. Steve Jobs, Bill Gates, and Mark Zuckerberg all dropped out of college. Based on their level of education, all three should have fallen into the $50,401 per year household income range.

In such an accomplished group of entrepreneurs, education didn't seem to carry the same gravitas. They aren't the only ones. Because he so profoundly believed that receiving a college education was antiquated and unnecessary, PayPal cofounder Peter Thiel once offered $100,000 scholarships to students if they *dropped out* of college.[27]

Jobs, Gates, and Zuckerberg weren't the only ones to evade the "guaranteed" earnings of a college education. Michael Dell of Dell Computers dropped out of college at an uneducated nineteen. Larry Ellison, founder of Oracle, dropped out of medical school. The list goes on and on. Are these übersuccessful individuals just outliers? While there are many other school dropouts who weren't as successful, these outliers successfully challenged the linearity of the success-education relationship.

This education end run isn't just reserved for tech entrepreneurs. Rappers Jay-Z and Drake, golfer Tiger Woods, actor Leonardo DiCaprio, and actress Whoopi Goldberg all left the guaranteed return of higher education to take a shot at greatness. This isn't to say that every MIT student should drop out. The point here is to understand how our assumptions about what is necessary for success are often incomplete.

Our view of education is predictable and comfortable. It's natural to believe that the more education you get, the better you'll do. And

---

26 "Learn More, Earn More: Education Leads to Higher Wages, Lower Unemployment," U.S. Bureau of Labor Statistics, May 2020, https://www.bls.gov/careeroutlook/2020/data-on-display/education-pays.htm.

27 "Two Years. $100,000. Some Ideas Can't Wait," Thiel Fellowship, accessed June 18, 2024, https://thielfellowship.org/.

for the most part, that's true. However, Michael Dell, Jay-Z, and Whoopi Goldberg challenged that calculus. It would appear that higher education also suffers from another unexpected paradox.

The Statista income data on degrees to earnings was based on medians—data representing the middle of the pack. This calculus makes sense if we're looking for average or even above average. But greatness? When we are looking for greatness, that linear process fails miserably. Greatness is much more elusive.

Don't believe me? Let's look at the top twenty CEOs on the 2020 Fortune 500 list and the corresponding college where they attained their first degree.[28]

---

28 "Fortune 500," *Fortune*, December 18, 2023, https://fortune.com/ranking/fortune500/2020/.

CHAPTER 7

CEO	Company	University Degree
Doug McMillon	Walmart	University of Arkansas
Darren Woods	Exxon Mobil	Texas A&M University
Tim Cook	Apple	Auburn University
Warren Buffett	Berkshire Hathaway	University of Nebraska
Jeff Bezos	Amazon	Princeton University
David Wichmann	United Health	Illinois State University
Bryan S. Tyler	McKesson	University of California, Santa Cruz
Larry Merlo	CVS Health	University of Pittsburgh
Randall Stephenson	AT&T	University of Central Oklahoma
Steven Collis	Amerisource	University of Witwatersrand
Mike Wirth	Chevron	University of Colorado
James Hackett	Ford	University of Michigan
Mary Barra	General Motors	Kettering University
Craig Jelinek	Costco	San Diego State
Sundar Pichai	Google	Indian Institute of Technology
Mike Kaufmann	Cardinal Health	Ohio Northern University
Stefano Pessina	Walgreens	Polytechnic University of Milan
Jamie Dimon	JP Morgan Chase	Tufts University
Hans Vestberg	Verizon	Uppsala University
Rodney McMullen	Kroger	University of Kentucky

39

This list includes many of the world's most successful CEOs. Theoretically, it should be riddled with Ivy League graduates. Jeff Bezos graduated from Princeton, but that's it. No other Ivy League graduates grace this list. If the relationship between greatness and educational investment were linear and predictable, most of these CEOs would have graduated from the most expensive elite schools. If that were true, why is San Diego State—with a nominal annual tuition of just $7,720—on this list?

Some would argue that a CEO career is only one incomplete measure of an Ivy League investment. What if there was a way to evaluate the financial investment and return from an Ivy League education? In a study published in Investopedia, Adam P. Brownlee asked just that: "Is an Ivy League Degree Worthwhile?" He writes,[29]

> Our discounted cash flow model delivers a resounding no. According to this model, an individual is much better off value-wise to attend a public school as they can expect to receive a much higher return based on their invested tuition and fees.

Specially, the results show that public schools have a net present value—the present value of cash inflows and outflows over a period of time—that's over $200,000 more than Ivy League schools, with a rate of return that is almost 7 percent higher. This is clearly a paradox!

While students agonize over SAT scores, hire tutors, and struggle to prepare an Ivy League–worthy application, the evidence doesn't necessarily support that astronomical investment. This miscalculation doesn't only burden our youth with the compulsion to attend these

---

29 Adam P. Brownlee, "Is an Ivy League Degree Worthwhile?" Investopedia, updated February 8, 2023, https://www.investopedia.com/articles/personal-finance/112815/ivy-league-degree-worth-it.asp.

schools by any means necessary; it also inappropriately imbues the Ivy elite with pseudosuperhuman talents.

Don't get me wrong, an Ivy League education is top notch. I'm simply saying that other pathways to achieve exist. Like my executive coach, we often jump to conclusions. While those conclusions are made in good faith, they're made with a limited view—even if those views are commonly held.

The school one attends is an important predictor of future success, but it's only one factor in an individual's total success picture. What school they chose to attend isn't as important as how they performed at the school they chose to attend. And there are other questions too. What else did they do while they were there? Were they in student government? Did they play a sport? Did they have a job to help pay their tuition? We must assess grit and character and all those other factors that tell us more than the school they graduated from.

It's much more difficult to make predictions for individuals who didn't attend Ivy League schools than it is to accept that Ivy League graduates are destined for greatness. Paradoxically, that mindset would have missed every top twenty Fortune 500 CEO except one.

Whether we're coaching future executives or supporting the dreams of our children, this is the trap we can easily fall into. We're susceptible to what we believe is standard, accepted, and appropriate. We believe we know who is "right" for the job because we settle for what is comfortable and superficial. But if we look closely, instead of simply accepting the consensus convention, we may find the faulty "O-rings" in this mindset.

Finding the right fit for one's education is a far more successful plan than assuming that one particular grouping of universities will guarantee an outcome. That determination is tedious and, at times, overbearing, but in the end, it will be far more fruitful. If we challenge

LESS THAN ONE PERCENT

our conventional wisdom, we'll find that greatness can emerge from any corner of the academic world. It may take a little more effort on our part, but it's more than worth it.

CHAPTER 8

FALLACIES

Fallacies do not cease to be fallacies because they become fashions.

–G. K. Chesterton

Doting parents aren't only committed to their burgeoning young academics; they also support young athletes with the same devoted ferocity. Almost every elementary school superstar athlete—or at least every parent of every elementary school superstar athlete—dreams of the possibility of becoming a professional athlete. The beauty of starting a six-year-old in the sport of their choice is that the possibilities are infinite. This array of potential potentials is precisely why parents scream at the top of their lungs on the sidelines, almost come to blows in the stands, and refinance their homes looking for an athletic return on investment.

Parenting is a job filled with imagination and optimism, and being the parent of an enterprising young athlete expands that optimism to new heights. This parental overexuberance occurs because when kids are young, parents believe their children can be and do anything. After all, isn't that what good parenting is all about?

The farther off the future is, the greater the potential possibilities. And when it comes to sports, that potential optimism manifests in the form of elementary professional athletes. No one would ever be overcritical of a parent who is overcommitted to their child's interests. That helicoptering not only dictates the intensity of that commitment, but it also determines what sports parents encourage their kids to pursue.

Arguably, America may have the most magnificent assortment of athletes in the world. While it may be an oversimplification to compare countries athletically, America has an impressive track record. With respect to the sheer number of athletes and their performance on the world stage, Americans dominate.

That dominance is more than evident every four years, when countries collectively compare their athletes at the Olympics. As an individual spectacle, the Olympics boast the most comprehensive combination of international athletic contests in the world. Performance at the Olympics highlights a country's athletic infrastructure, but it also highlights its relative number and quality of athletes.

As a metric, Olympic medal count is an excellent proxy for a country's athletic stature. If we look at the data in the following chart, some themes stand out. Bigger countries mostly outperform smaller ones; richer countries often outperform poorer ones. Because of those themes, America is uniquely advantaged to excel in this 127-year-old contest.

It's obvious from the total Olympic medal data that the United States has the highest number of high-performing athletes in the world. American athletes shine on the international stage, and they also stand out in sports such as American football and basketball.[30]

Country	Total Olympic Medals
United States	2,980
United Kingdom	948
Germany	892
France	874
Italy	742
China	696
Sweden	661
Australia	562
Japan	555
Russia	547

Given the financial windfall that can accompany athletic success, American youth athletics is a highly incentivized gig. The astronomical, generationally changing salaries provide more than enough incentive for young aspiring athletes to "be like Mike!"

When most kids and their families dream about the careers burgeoning stars can have, they often envision the enormous salaries offered by the NBA and the NFL. With these potential financial windfalls and its overall athletic supremacy, America should be

---

30 "Olympic Medals by Country," Data Pandas, accessed June 18, 2024, https://www.datapandas.org/ranking/olympic-medals-by-country.

dominant in just about every sport. And that is true except for the world's most popular sport—soccer.

Soccer—a term derived from "assocer," which is slang for the English Football Association—is an unfortunate black eye on America's athletic résumé. Analysts have postulated several hypotheses to explain America's underwhelming soccer history and perpetual inferior performance. Some say America doesn't have enough quality coaches. Others say American children don't have the same early childhood training rigor as other soccer-dominant countries.

While the reason for America's paltry performance is unclear, its lack of success relative to its infrastructure and population makes its understated performance an understatement. In a country with all the access and all the athletes and all the financial wherewithal, there is no reasonable explanation for this conundrum. It feels like one plus one equals three. It feels a little like a paradox.

As little kids shoot fadeaway jump shots in their driveways, work on their throwing form, and take batting practice in the backyard, they're investing in professional careers that have the potential to yield life-changing incomes. If you were to watch ESPN—America's most popular sports news network—you would see why basketball, football, and baseball are the most popular sports in America. Every dunk-filled commercial, home run–belting advertisement, and bone-crushing tackle highlights the fact that success in these sports can turn an athlete into an overnight celebrity. And with that celebrity status comes the spoils.

Between expensive athletic scholarships and potential future multimillion-dollar endorsements, young students can quickly turn a passionate hobby into a lucrative career. American sports, predominantly made up of football, baseball, basketball, and hockey, can earn their organizers billions. In 2022 alone, football's champion contest garnered over $500 million in advertising revenue.

Football, baseball, and basketball are woven into America's cultural fabric. LeBron James and Steph Curry, Tom Brady and Russell Wilson, Vladimir Guerrero Jr., and Mike Trout are names kids idolize. And what of other sports? It's difficult for young American athletes to envision a return on their investment from less popular sports. Soccer is one of those sports. If you're a soccer fan, you know what's coming next.

By revenue, the NFL is the richest sports organization in the world, followed by Major League Baseball, and then the NBA.[31] Here is where it gets a little interesting. If you sorted the top ten sports leagues in the world, the largest revenue earner would be soccer. What's more, if you were to rank each sport based on a worldwide fan base, soccer wins in a landslide!

What Americans call soccer, the world more appropriately calls football—a sport that has four billion fans worldwide. Almost half of the world's inhabitants are soccer fans! Is American football second? Not even close! Soccer is followed by cricket at 2.5 billion fans, and then hockey and tennis. Basketball is a distant seventh at 825 million fans. American football isn't even in the top ten.[32]

Maybe it's about more than popularity. Although popular American sports have smaller fan bases than international soccer, their individual salaries are assumed to be far greater than those in international football. But that assumption would be wrong.

---

31 Kevin Omuya and Jackline Wangare, "Which Are the 15 Richest Sports Leagues in the World Currently?" Sports Brief, updated February 13, 2024, https://sportsbrief.com/other-sports/32109-which-richest-sports-leagues-world-currently/.

32 SportyTell Editors, "Top-10 Most Popular Sports in the World 2023," SportyTell, updated July 4, 2023, https://sportytell.com/sports/most-popular-sports-world/.

LESS THAN ONE PERCENT

In 2021 the world's highest-earning athlete wasn't a basketball, football, or baseball player. The highest-earning athlete in 2021 was an English Football Association (soccer) player named Lionel Messi. The good news for burgeoning young basketball players is that LeBron James was second overall. LeBron was then followed by Cristiano Ronaldo and another soccer player, Neymar da Silva Santos Júnior. Between endorsements and actual salary, three of the top four highest-earning athletes are soccer players. If we remove endorsements, soccer players were the top three richest athletes in 2021.[33]

This is what we call a fallacy. A fallacy is a mistaken belief, especially one based on an unsound argument. Kids and parents invest their time into sports discipline because they enjoy it. While they don't always participate in their sport of choice to make millions, they still gravitate to what's popular. Unfortunately, in America, soccer isn't popular.

America's soccer problem is even more evident when we examine the international soccer results. The World Cup, administered by the Federation of International Football Association (FIFA), is the world's most prestigious soccer spectacle. Compared with America's array of Olympic medals in almost every other sport, their World Cup results are downright anemic.[34]

---

[33] Scooby Axson, "Lionel Messi, LeBron James Tops Forbes' List of Highest-Paid Athletes," *USA Today*, May 18, 2022, https://www.usatoday.com/story/sports/2022/05/18/lionel-messi-lebron-james-highest-paid-athletes/9820690002/.

[34] Ed Farnsworth, "USMNT Results," Society for American Soccer History, accessed June 18, 2024, https://www.ussoccerhistory.org/usnt-results/usmnt-results/.

World Cup	United States Result
Brazil 1950	Group stage
Switzerland 1954	Did not qualify
Sweden 1958	Did not qualify
Chile 1962	Did not qualify
England 1966	Did not qualify
Mexico 1970	Did not qualify
West Germany 1974	Did not qualify
Argentina 1978	Did not qualify
Spain 1982	Did not qualify
Mexico 1986	Did not qualify
Italy 1990	Group stage
United States 1994	Round of 16
France 1998	Group stage
South Korea/Japan 2002	Quarterfinals
Germany 2006	Group stage
South Africa 2010	Round of 16
Brazil 2014	15th
Russia 2018	Did not qualify

Between 1950 and 2022, the men's national team made it to the round of sixteen or beyond only in five of the last nineteen World Cups. The best result they could muster was a quarterfinal finish in South Korea. Do you remember America's Olympic medal count? The men's soccer team hasn't contributed to that lofty count since they medaled in 1904! Between 2004 and 2020, they only qualified for the medal round once.[35]

Olympics Football Tournaments	United States Result
Spain 1992	9th
United States 1996	10th
Australia 2000	4th
Greece 2004	Did not qualify
China 2008	9th
United Kingdom 2012	Did not qualify
Brazil 2016	Did not qualify
Japan 2020	Did not qualify

America's individual player performances are just as unfortunate. Landon Donovan, who played in two World Cups, is America's most prolific scorer with five career goals. Bert Patenaude and Clint Dempsey scored four goals each in their long World Cup careers. Brian McBride was America's next with three, and twenty-one other players had scored a single goal each. America's most prolific scorers

---

35 Farnsworth, "USMNT Results."

haven't even scored one-third as many goals as Miroslav Klose from Germany, who leads the pack.[36]

Player	Career World Cup Goals	Team
Miroslav Klose	16	Germany
Ronaldo de Lima	15	Brazil
Gerd Müller	14	West Germany
Just Fontaine	13	France
Pelé	12	Brazil
Sándor Kocsis	11	Hungary
Jürgen Klinsmann	11	Germany
Helmut Rahn	10	West Germany
Gary Lineker	10	England
Gabriel Batistuta	10	Argentina
Teófilo Cubillas	10	Peru
Thomas Müller	10	Germany
Grzegorz Lato	10	Poland
Eusébio	9	Portugal
Christian Vieri	9	Italy

36 "World Cup All-Time Topscorers," Worldfootball.net, accessed June 18, 2024, https://www.worldfootball.net/alltime_goalgetter/wm/tore/1/.

LESS THAN ONE PERCENT

In a part of the world that produces so many elite athletes, where are America's elite soccer players? Not only are the best American soccer players not playing in the World Cup, but the best American soccer players aren't even playing soccer. Athletes with the potential to overachieve in soccer play football, basketball, and baseball.

LeBron James is arguably one of the best athletes in American history. LeBron is six foot nine with a wingspan of more than seven feet. He also boasts a forty-four-inch vertical leap—one of the highest in the NBA. His eight-and-a-half feet is six inches higher than the top of the soccer goal. If you add his vertical leap, he clears the top of the goal by more than three feet.

With his range, length, athleticism, and jumping ability, LeBron could have been the greatest goaltender in American history. Of course, LeBron's impact on basketball is likely second only to Michael Jeffrey Jordan. However, for soccer's sake, the United States may have missed out on one of the best ever.

If you are playing basketball, football, or baseball for the love of the game, then go for it. Be the best player you can be. But if you plan to perfect your craft to make millions as a professional athlete, soccer may be your best bet. The argument for soccer is more compelling if you consider the numbers for young American athletes.

In the 2021–2022 high school season, 521,616 boys and 370,466 girls played high school basketball.[37] Each year the NBA drafts ninety players worldwide. That's a success ratio of 0.017 percent. Each season the Women's National Basketball Association (WNBA) drafts thirty-six players. For aspiring young girls, the odds of playing professional basketball in the WNBA are a slim 0.010 percent.[38]

---

[37] "Number of Participants in High School Basketball in the United States from 2010/2011 to 2021/2022, by Gender," Statista, December 8, 2022, https://www.statista.com/statistics/267942/participation-in-us-high-school-basketball/.

[38] Statista, "Number of Participants in High School Basketball in the United States."

CHAPTER 8

Soccer participation at the high school level in America isn't as dire as the men's national team's record might suggest. After all, 800,000 high school boys and girls play the game each year.[39] It's estimated that there are approximately 130,000 professional soccer players worldwide.[40] The odds of becoming an international soccer star are far greater than the odds of playing professional basketball. At least from a mathematical perspective, soccer is a better professional bet.

The one bright spot for American soccer is America's national women's team. They haven't just fared better than their male counterparts; they've also been downright dominant. America's women have medaled in almost every Olympics and have dominated in the FIFA Women's World Cup. The performance gap between the two teams is perplexing until we closely examine the data.

Over 32 percent of all American female high school athletes play soccer. For high school boys, it's an entirely different story. High school boys don't play soccer at the same rate as high school girls. Most prefer football, track, basketball, and baseball. Even with all the worldwide popularity, and the highest financial return in the world, American boys don't care much for soccer.[41]

The reason we should identify fallacies isn't to change one's mind or opinion. The reason we should identify fallacies is to be open to changing one's mind or opinion. Once we've identified a fallacy, we can begin to understand the premature assumptions and unfounded

---

39 "Soccer in the U.S.—Statistics & Facts," Statista, December 18, 2023, https://www.statista.com/topics/2780/soccer-in-the-us/#topicOverview.

40 Connor Smith, "How Many Soccer Players in the World?" SoccerPrime, accessed June 18, 2024, https://soccerprime.com/how-many-soccer-players-in-the-world/.

41 "Number of Participants in High School Soccer in the United States from 2010/2011 to 2021/2022, by Gender," Statista, December 8, 2022, https://www.statista.com/statistics/267963/participation-in-us-high-school-soccer/.

arguments that color our vision. After all, results are results. America's World Cup performances speak for themselves.

These outcomes could be attributed to any number of things, including a lack of coaching or the absence of European-like "football association" infrastructure. But if we look closer, we'll find a deeper potential explanation. If the United States ever hopes to match its soccer prowess with the success of its other sports, the key will be finding a way to make soccer popular among young American boys.

The solutions to America's soccer performance problem—and likely many other social conundrums—lie in the space between what we believe we know and what's actually true. It's in this space that fallacies reside and paradoxes propagate. It's where we inappropriately create rules from conventions and where we double down on our faith that one plus one equals three. It's a space where parents overvalue an overvalued education, where emergency physicians see patients one at a time, and where high school basketball players are anointed far too early. It's a space where the expertise of experts is fatally overwhelmed by the need for consensus.

That narrow gap in understanding leads us to choose the winners and losers before we even understand the rules of the game. Hopefully, understanding America's soccer conundrum got us a little closer to understanding that space. And if not, the United States women's national soccer team likely has the answer.

CHAPTER 9

BARRY O'SHEA

> *When 99% of people doubt your idea, you're either gravely wrong or about to make history.*
>
> –Scott Belsky

True greatness requires someone in your corner—an advocate who will not only push you but will also allow you to learn and grow through your mistakes. Without Coach McKillop, Steph Curry would never have become Steph Curry. Whether it's a mentor, coach, or teacher, there's always someone whose purpose is to catalyze another's greatness equation.

Having someone in your corner can be wonderfully motivating. But people cheering against you can often be far more motivating. Someone saying "you can" is motivating, but someone saying "you can't" may be even more powerful. Telling a potential chief executive officer candidate that they have less than a one percent chance of becoming a chief executive officer is an unwitting invitation to overachieve. It doesn't always have to be something so obvious. Sometimes, even the smallest of slights can send someone careening toward greatness.

Honestly, before my coach presented me with such dismal odds, being a CEO wasn't even on my career radar. Whether he meant it or not, it felt like an obvious and purposeful slight. Or so I believed.

The slight I felt wasn't because I wanted to be a CEO. The slight I felt was because my coach believed I couldn't be a CEO—not shouldn't or wouldn't but couldn't. The difference between wouldn't and couldn't is subtle but powerful. The idea that he didn't believe I could was even more motivating than if he believed I could. His doubt made me fanatical about proving him gravely wrong.

In my book *Maniacal Fanaticism,* I talk about the inward chip. The inward chip is an internal doubt that drives Maniacal Fanatics to succeed. In some individuals, self-doubt can be debilitating. It can lead to second-guessing, insecurity, and a general lack of confidence. However, for a subset of the population—if directed inward—self-doubt can be uplifting and inspire unparalleled performance.

Self-doubt comes from a place of humility. When managed internally, that introspective secret doubt can heighten performance. That performance is self-driven, sustained, and can exist without an external motivator. External doubt is an entirely different thing. It relies on anger and resentment and can spark otherwise otherworldly performances.

Pursuing greatness isn't your average response to being doubted. Coach McKillop pushed Steph Curry, but he didn't tell Steph he would never be the greatest shooter of all time. It takes a particular personality type to turn a negative prediction into the opposite result. This quality is unique to less-than-one-percenters, and it's counter to the way most people typically respond to negative events. This unique behavior challenges conventions and exposes paradoxes.

CHAPTER 9

These perceived slights don't last a few months or years. Many people carry them for a lifetime. And for me, it all started with Barry O'Shea. I'm not surprised if the name Barry O'Shea doesn't ring a bell. Barry O'Shea isn't a celebrity, world-class athlete, or Fortune 500 CEO. Barry was my former teammate, and I'll never forget his impact on me.

Barry may not know this, but he has motivated me beyond our high fives and schoolyard conversations. He was what I call a participator. He was that kid who joined every team. He played basketball and volleyball and was on the track team. We didn't have American football, so most of the boys played rugby. Of course, Barry played that too.

While I can remember Barry O'Shea being a part of just about every team, I can't remember what role he played on any of those teams. I remember one year in particular. I was the most valuable player in soccer and basketball. We won the city championship in volleyball, and I was second in the city in the one-hundred-meter and four-hundred-meter dashes. It was a fantastic year, and I proudly represented my school. Then the unthinkable happened.

All the athletes sat together, more forced than a result of our collective camaraderie. Assemblies are painful, but far less painful than being in class. You can imagine the level of overcompetition at an all-boys school. There is something about wearing a blazer and tie every day that makes after-school sports that much more disagreeable.

But after all, this was a ceremony, and everybody was on their best behavior. Mostly because compliance avoided "JUGS"—an acronym that the monks used to describe after-school detention—which translated to "Judgement Under God." Whether academically or athletically, competitive environments are tactlessly full of judgment.

Achieving something because you want to be the best is more than enough motivation, but sometimes, it feels good to be recognized. Soon-to-be adult boys are particularly sensitive to their coaches and teachers recognizing their accomplishments. Each sport has its top athlete. The ideal teammate is one who's talented, produces, and makes their teammates better. That premise holds true in sports, family, and business.

Ultimately, the most respected of all athletes is one whose contributions transcend all sports. An athlete whose aptitude, talent, and skill allow them to deliver irrespective of the sport or situation. That manifestation culminates in the valedictorian of sports performance or the athlete of athletes. After the smaller and sports-specific accolades were handed out, everyone awaited the final and most coveted award. Though antsy, every young man sat perfectly still as the athletic director said those words. "This year's athlete of the year is …"

"Barry O'Shea!"

Rage was too tame of emotion to describe my initial feeling, and the associated nausea made it even worse. That was the moment Barry O'Shea became one of my greatest motivations. That moment is forever etched in my memory. When I'm tired, overworked, angry, sad, or unmotivated, two words keep me focused. Those two words are Barry O'Shea.

Motivation may be internal, but external doubt can fire up that internal response. It fuels a compulsion to prove the 99 percent wrong. That's precisely how paradoxes are disrupted and how conventions are broken. Barry O'Shea unwittingly helped unearth something inside me. And that feeling helped create my CEO paradox. Hearing the word "couldn't" from a coach whose supposed purpose was to get the best out of me was like hearing "Barry O'Shea" all over again.

This isn't an altogether new concept. The "prove you wrong" narrative has existed for years. Many people talk about being "doubted," especially when they don't get the credit they believe they deserve. What's the difference? Not only do the less-than-one-percenters carry that insult for longer than others, but they also overreact. This overreaction occurs in the area of the slight, and it also takes over other areas of their lives.

This overreaction and overcompensation lead to overpreparation and overwork, resulting in improved overperformance. It becomes a compulsion. They come early. They stay late. They work harder because someone told them they couldn't. It comes from a place of anger and insolence. Fortunately, these traditionally negative feelings coalesce to produce positive results. It's an obsession that inspires people who can't to become people who can.

Being slighted isn't a good thing, but good things often come from being slighted. In many ways it can be a more powerful motivator than being supported. But converting all that negative energy into positive outcomes comes at a cost. There is a fine line between carrying a slight that is motivating and carrying a slight that is debilitating. For me, Barry O'Shea became a compulsion. His name became an obsession. Every time I visited my high school, I would find the plaque with his name on it. Years later it still elicited the same rage and nausea.

While that may seem a little intense, holding on to these kinds of perceived slights isn't all that rare. Maybe the greatest of all time at harboring these slights is also the greatest of all time at basketball. Michael Jordan made a career of holding on to slights—some perceived and some real. He used what would otherwise be considered innocuous to fuel his focus and performance. For individuals such as

Michael Jordan, just about anything—and almost everything—can become a slight.

Michael Jordan's reaction to perceived slights was well chronicled in *The Last Dance*, a documentary about his final season and sixth championship with the Chicago Bulls. During the 1996 NBA final, Jordan walked into a restaurant and saw George Karl, head coach of the opposing team. Karl didn't greet Jordan. It's unclear if he ignored Jordan or simply didn't see him. Nevertheless, as described in *The Last Dance*, Jordan was incensed: "He walked right past me.... Really. Oh, that's how you're going to play it.... We went to Carolina, we know Dean Smith, I've seen him in the summer. We play golf.... That's all I needed."

Jordan's "that's all I needed" comment makes it clear that he's a less-than-one-percenter. A perceived slight was all he needed to catalyze his motivation, refine his focus, and execute. What did that execution look like? Jordan scored over twenty-seven points in that series, knocking George Karl and his Seattle SuperSonics out of the playoffs. Jordan dominated the series, all while carrying that slight in the back or, in his case, in the front of his mind. But this wasn't an isolated incident. Throughout his storied career, he sought out these slights and used them to enhance his performance.

This wasn't the first perceived slight of Jordan's career. It was one in a litany of "Barry O'Shea" moments. Jordan often talked about not being chosen to play on his high school varsity team as a sophomore. That slight burned so deeply that he still brought it up decades later. Jordan was also left off a *Sports Illustrated* cover that highlighted four of his North Carolina teammates. While these slights weren't responsible for Jordan's success, he was wired in such a way that seared these slights into his psyche. And he used them as motivation to achieve even more.

For Michael Jordan, these slights were a powerful motivator. The bigger the slight, the bigger the motivation—at least at first. As time passed, one would assume that Jordan's motivation would wane. Not only did his motivation increase in response to older and newer slights, but the level of slight that could elicit his motivational response also decreased. Jordan not only responded in kind to large and overtly offensive slights, but he also reacted with the same veracity to insignificant slights.

My initial reaction to the Barry O'Shea slight was understandable. Most kids in that situation would be disappointed, angry, and confused. That appropriate initial reaction to that insult eventually became a disproportionate overreaction. The Barry O'Shea slight became my everyday slight, which became my CEO slight, which became my every-time-they-doubt-me slight. And for every small and insignificant slight, I had the same overwhelming reaction that I had with the original slight. When I heard "less than one percent," I heard "Barry O'Shea."

This isn't to say we should go into the world finding and holding grudges. I'm simply saying that a subset of people find inspiration in a world that doesn't believe in their greatness. Emotions that should deflate and deter counterintuitively serve to inspire—a process catalyzed exponentially by each consecutive slight.

Ironically, whether it was purposeful or not, my coach's doubt ignited a fire in me—a fire that resulted in an unforeseen outcome. It took anger and insolence to disrupt an arbitrary and nebulous CEO standard. "Underrated" Steph Curry became the superstar Steph Curry because someone believed in him. I became a CEO because someone didn't believe in me. Although I hate to admit it, I would have never become the CEO of a multibillion-dollar company without Barry O'Shea.

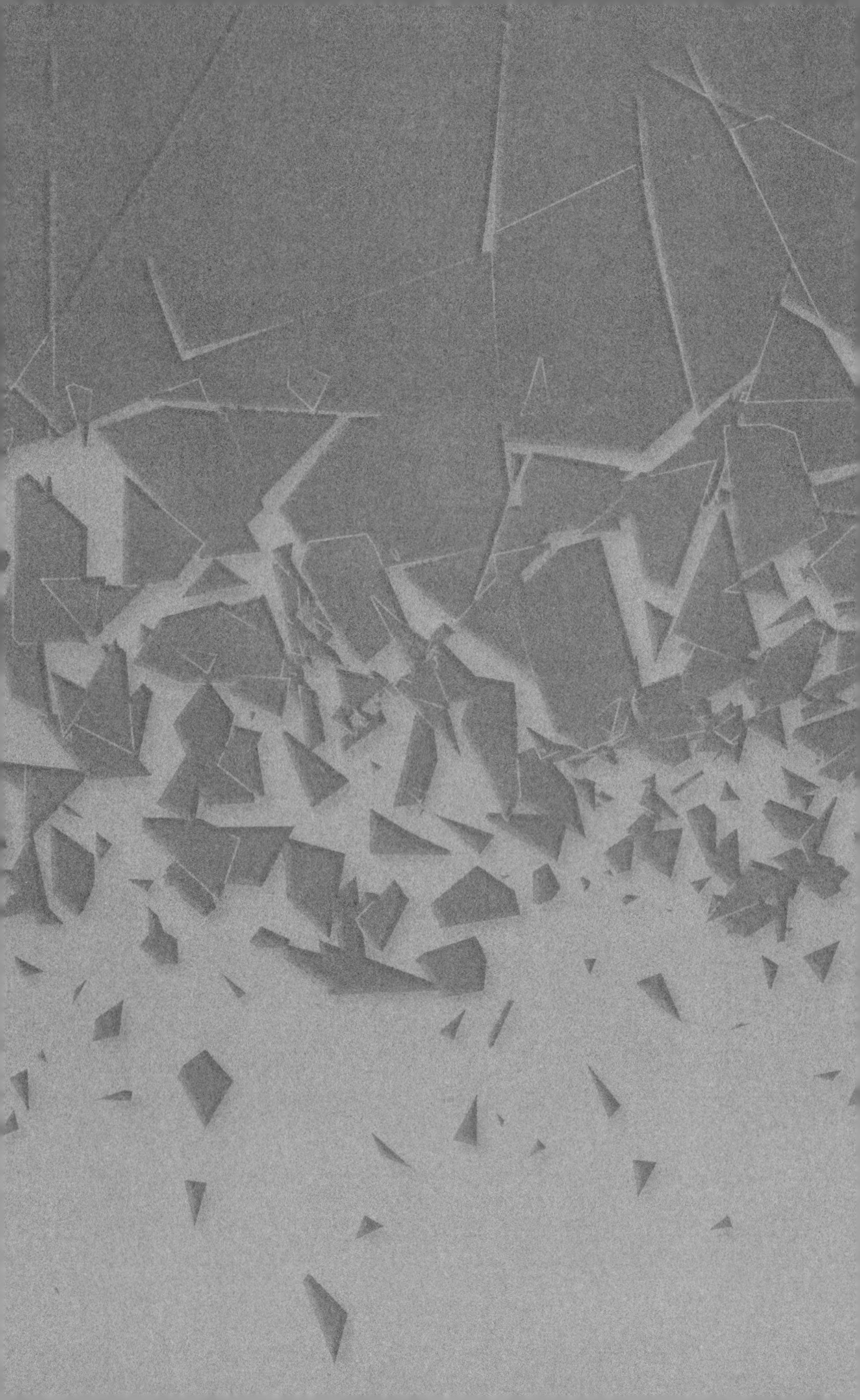

CHAPTER 10

WI LIKKLE BUT WI TALLAWAH

By not wanting to be wrong, we are usually wrong.

—Imamu Tomlinson

In 2009 no Jamaican had ever won a world title in the one-hundred-meter dash. Although Usain Bolt won Jamaica's first one-hundred-meter Olympic gold medal in 2008, no Jamaican had ever won the World Championships in the one-hundred-meter dash. At the 2009 World Athletics Championships in Berlin, two Jamaicans were favored to break that barrier. But there was also an American trying to make his own history.

The three fastest men in the world lined up: Jamaica's Usain Bolt, who ran his last one-hundred-meter dash and set a world record at 9.6 seconds; Jamaica's Asafa Powell, who last ran the one-hundred-meter dash in 9.7 seconds; and American Tyson Gay, who also ran his last race at 9.7 seconds. This spectacle didn't just feature three of the fastest men at the time. It featured three of the fastest men of *all* time.

If you aren't a track enthusiast, it's hard to describe the grind that is the one-hundred-meter dash. These three gentlemen had already run three grueling heats—preliminary races that are used to narrow the field to the eight final runners. What makes it even worse is many sprinters also participate in other events during the course of a track meet.

The one-hundred-meter dash is not only about speed, but it's also about strategy, endurance, and resilience. In a contest of millimeters and milliseconds, every ounce of preparation and mental fortitude can affect an outcome. In a race that lasts only ten seconds at best, strategic adjustments during each race are almost impossible.

"Bang!" Without warning, the gun went off. Bolt, a notoriously poor starter who liked to start from behind, got off to an uncharacteristically fantastic start. All three frontrunners looked synchronized, running stride for stride while ignoring the rest of the pack. The only difference between the three was that Bolt's six-foot-five frame covered far more ground than his two shorter competitors.

Bolt's stride was elegant. If you only looked at how he ran—his style and effort—you would have assumed he was dead last. He didn't look like he ran the fastest, but he ran the fastest. And nonchalantly blew away the competition. Nine and a half seconds later, he strolled to another new world record.

His Olympic world record performance in 2008 was even more impressive because he also dominated the 200-meter and the 4 × 100-meter relay. Bolt is the only sprinter in history to win the 100-meter and 200-meter races in three consecutive Olympics (2008, 2012, and 2016). Bolt became one of the most decorated and dominant Jamaican sprinters in history. More than that, Bolt became the most dominant sprinter in the world.[42]

There is more to Bolt's record-breaking win than just the miracle of an unrivaled athletic performance. His dominant performance was a paradox. Bolt was awkwardly tall for a sprinter. His teammate Asafa Powell was three inches shorter, and his American counterpart was shorter still at five foot eleven.

Bolt stood out because of his length and stride, but these traits weren't historically attributed to successful short-distance sprinters. A *Journal of Sports Science and Medicine* study found that world champion sprinters ranged between five foot nine at the low end and six foot three at the absolute max.[43] Six foot three at the absolute max? Bolt is a conservative six foot five![44]

---

42   Utathya Nag, "Usain Bolt's Records: Best Strikes from the Lightning Bolt," Olympics.com, October 12, 2020, https://olympics.com/en/news/usain-bolt-record-world-champion-athlete-fastest-man-olympics-sprinter-100m-200m.

43   Edward Mcclelland, "Taking Sprinting to New Heights," *Slate*, August 20, 2009, https://slate.com/news-and-politics/2009/08/why-haven-t-there-been-more-tall-sprinters-like-usain-bolt.html.

44   "World Record Progression of 100 Metres," World Athletics, accessed June 21, 2024, https://worldathletics.org/records/by-progression/16647.

Olympic Year	100m Gold Medalist	Height
2016	Usain Bolt	6'5"
2012	Usain Bolt	6'5"
2008	Usain Bolt	6'5"
2004	Justin Gatlin	6'1"
2000	Maurice Green	5'9"
1996	Donovan Bailey	6'1"
1992	Linford Christie	6'2"
1988	Carl Lewis	6'2"
1984	Carl Lewis	6'2"

Based on track conventions, Usain Bolt shouldn't have come close to breaking a world record. If sprinters of the past were the standard, Bolt shouldn't have beaten anyone. His world record performance threw the sports physiology world into a tizzy. His performance compelled the track establishment to analyze every microsecond of his races.

How did Bolt, who exceeded the six-foot-three max, compete as a short-distance sprinter? Where did the track science world miscalculate? They miscalculated by trying to understand how he could compete at his height rather than trying to understand how others couldn't compete with him at his height. Their analysis focused on the competitive disadvantages of his height rather than the competitive advantages of his height.

CHAPTER 10

The one-hundred-meter dash is usually about speed, but Bolt made the race about speed *and* distance. His taller frame and longer legs meant that he didn't have to run as fast as his shorter competitors. Ironically, most of his competitors were moving their legs faster than he was.

Bolt's stride rate—the number of strides it takes to complete the one hundred meters—averaged about forty-one. The rest of the field averaged approximately forty-five strides. Because of the comparatively longer length of each stride, Bolt required four fewer strides to travel the same one hundred meters. His stride frequency—the number of strides per second—was comparatively lower than his competitors.[45]

Paradoxically, he didn't "run" the fastest, but he was the first to cross the finish line. Before Bolt, taller sprinters were discouraged from running the one-hundred-meter because of their slower stride rates. Additionally, taller runners generate more drag—the resistance a runner's frame generates. Bolt's stride efficiency offset the drag of his larger frame. In doing so, he disrupted the prevailing taller-sprinter science of that time. He created a one-hundred-meter paradox.

When it comes to picking winners and losers, track is decidedly mathematical. Track is the ultimate meritocracy. There's no need to debate. The runners line up, the gun goes off, and the first person to cross the finish line wins. No need for consensus-driven evaluators or groupthink committee votes to unobjectively postulate who the fastest could be.

If basketball were structured more like track athletics, Steph Curry's 256th ranking would have been solely based on results, not arbitrary measures of "upside." Relying on objective results makes it unlikely that there could ever be a paradox or fallacy in track—especially in the one-hundred-meter sprint. But there's so much that we

---

[45] "Technique: Analysis of Usain Bolt's Running Technique," Pose Method, July 7, 2015, https://posemethod.com/usain-bolts-running-technique/.

don't see. Many consider Bolt to be an anomaly or categorize him as an outlier. In the history of the one-hundred-meter dash, he is a unique combination of speed and length, a combination that we have never seen. But why haven't we?

Bolt's unparalleled success tells us a lot about him, but it tells us even more about Jamaica. Track is Jamaica's number one sport.[46] Jamaica's entire high school athletic infrastructure is built around what has become its national sport. If you were to try to understand the intensity of the relationship between track and Jamaica, you would have to take all of the student athletes in multiple sports in America and have them first compete in track. If every school competed against every other school until the competitors were narrowed down to the top eight runners in the country, then those eight would race off to have one national winner. This is exactly what happens in Jamaica!

Every Jamaican student athlete competes with other athletes from their high school, who then compete against the best athletes in every other school. The competition intensifies by school and then by parish—similar to American counties. The competition culminates in a nationwide team competition, the Inter-Secondary Schools Boys and Girls Championship—more appropriately called "Champs."

Champs is the biggest and the most popular athletic competition in Jamaica.[47] Champs isn't just an athletic competition. It's more of a cultural event and occurs for five days. At the end of March, when this competition is typically held, Jamaica is literally at a standstill. The track meet is broadcast nationally in the thirty-five-thousand-seat National Stadium in Kingston, and not one seat is left open.

---

46 Jannik Lindner, "Statistics about the Most Popular Sports by Country," Gitnux, updated June 23, 2024, https://gitnux.org/most-popular-sports-by-country/.

47 Elena Dyachkova. "'Champs'—the Biggest Deal in Jamaica," World Athletics, April 8, 2014, https://worldathletics.org/news/feature/boys-girls-champs-jamaica-zharnel-hughes-issa.

CHAPTER 10

The crowd noise is deafening! Spectators scream at the top of their vocal range to support their high school. In a nation challenged by poverty and unemployment, high school can be a defining period for young Jamaicans. This is a time when students start to separate themselves academically. Many carry the honor of being accepted to the best high schools, while some are burdened with the stigma of being rejected.

Jamaicans are so closely tied to their high school that those badges stay with them for a lifetime. It isn't uncommon for Jamaicans in New York, Toronto, or Miami to get together based on the high school they attended. Connecting with other Jamaicans at a Rusea's or Manning's event is essentially a Jamaican ritual. And there is no place where that school spirit is more evident than at Champs.

While Jamaica's national athletics championship is run on an Olympic-style asphalt track, there are many smaller competitions that lead up to it. Many of those local and regional meets are held at schools that have grass tracks, and some of the athletes even run barefoot. It's been said that when you medal at Champs, there isn't a track in the world that can make you nervous or intimidate you.

Champs is so competitive that the future fastest man in Jamaican history could only muster a second place in the two-hundred-meter dash. Like many other future Olympians, Bolt used Champs to perfect his technique and hone his signature stride and bravado. After the Champs gauntlet, winning three consecutive Olympic gold medals may have seemed relatively easy.

In such an intensely competitive environment, having the right coach can make or break a sprinter's career. Fortunately, Bolt had his own version of Coach McKillop in his corner. Former Olympian Pablo recognized his speed while watching him playing cricket—one of Bolt's original favorite sports. Coach McNeil encouraged the long, lanky, and overly tall athlete to give sprinting a try.

Bolt's history is written. He is irrefutably the fastest man in the world. He is an anomaly, but characterizing him as an anomaly raises another question. How many other long, lanky, and overly tall athletes weren't encouraged to run track? Coach McNeil didn't just help Bolt become faster. He also encouraged Bolt to switch sports, trading cricket and soccer for track. Like Coach McKillop, Coach McNeil bucked the convention. He knew that Bolt's length wasn't a quality that would make him a better sprinter. He knew that Bolt's length was a quality that would make him a transcendent sprinter.

Even with Jamaica's dominance in track, Bolt was the first Jamaican sprinter to win the one-hundred-meter dash in history. His frame was an anomaly, and that frame allowed him to dominate year after year after year. Bolt was so unprecedently dominant that his winning percentage was 71 percent![48] That kind of winning percentage was unheard of in track.

But that begs the question, what if Bolt wasn't the first? What if other long, lanky, and overly tall sprinters had gotten the opportunity to decrease the number of strides it took to traverse one hundred meters? Bolt was fortunate enough to be the first to break convention and challenge the paradox. He was the first to challenge the shorter-short-distance-sprinter groupthink.

The Jamaican men aren't the only ones burning up the track. The Jamaican women have taken gold in the last four Olympic one-hundred-meter women's races. Elaine Thompson-Herah won in 2016 and 2020. Shelly-Ann Fraser-Pryce won in 2008 and 2012. Champs has produced seven of the last eight one-hundred-meter winners in the

---

48 "Usain Bolt," World Athletics, accessed June 19, 2024, https://worldathletics.org/athletes/jamaica/usain-bolt-14201847.

Olympics.[49] As impressive as Bolt is at six foot five, Shelly-Ann Fraser-Pryce is equally impressive for another reason—she is only five feet tall.

Still, Fraser-Pryce was able to beat five-foot-eleven Nigerian sprinter Blessing Okagbare. While stride length obviously isn't why a five-foot woman outsprints somebody almost a foot taller, Fraser-Pryce had a different advantage. Being low to the ground not only increases the number of strides you need to finish the one-hundred-meter dash, but it also helps sprinters start the race more efficiently. The time it takes to start from a low crouching position to a full standing sprint is significantly shorter for short sprinters. This advantage for Fraser-Pryce was the same disadvantage that Usain Bolt had to overcome. And that's just it!

Bolt broke the convention. He confused the track establishment. He created a new way of thinking about height, efficiency, and the physics of sprinting. But that doesn't mean we just create a new convention—by having all tall sprinters. Likewise, just because Fraser-Pryce has a markedly reduced start-to-sprint time doesn't mean we should create a convention around shorter sprinters.

The lesson here is that we should use that unique combination of strengths and weaknesses to maximize our chances of winning. And whenever we find ourselves on the short side (no pun intended) of a convention, we should always question that groupthink. Bolt was too tall to be a successful sprinter, and Fraser-Pryce was too short based on track standards. Standards are averages. They're recommendations. They're built on consensus and hardly ever account for exceptions. Greatness isn't standard. Greatness is an exception. And both Bolt and Fraser-Pryce capitalized on their unconventional exceptions.

---

49   Editors of *GQ*, "Inside 'Champs,' the Jamaican Track Meet That's Hiding the Next Usain Bolt," *GQ*, April 10, 2017, https://www.gq.com/story/jamaica-champs-track-photo-essay.

Fraser-Pryce also capitalized on Jamaica's track culture. She, too, was the fastest in her elementary school and was known for running barefoot. She attended Wolmer's High School and won the two-hundred-meter dash at Champs. The Fraser-Pryce story is eerily similar to the Bolt story. And their stories are remarkably similar to many other Jamaican sprinters. What appears to be a few unconventional individuals simply disproving a paradox is much more than that.

By not wanting to be wrong, we are usually wrong. We want so much to predict who has the right size and the right height and the right intelligence that we forget to identify the skills, traits, and characteristics that are truly responsible for an individual's success. We're often overconfident about what we *think* we know. We're also reticent to acknowledge what we don't know. It isn't necessarily that we want to be right about who will be successful. We just don't want to be wrong.

The process of attempting to avoid a success mistake leads directly to a success mistake. It's easier to focus on those we believe have a 99 percent chance of succeeding rather than trying to sift through the less than one percent—such as Fraser-Pryce and Bolt. Track coaches avoided training taller sprinters because they didn't want to be wrong. And in that process, they realized they were wrong.

Remember our Olympic medal data? Olympic medals serve as a measure of a country's athletic infrastructure and total number of athletes. The better a country's infrastructure and the higher a country's population, the higher the medal count. At least that's the theory.

Using this formula to analyze Jamaica's Olympic data, we find very intriguing results. If we calculate the number of summer gold medals per capita, Jamaica ranks seventh in the world, outperforming China, Russia, and even the United States of America. This little island, of approximately three million people with limited infrastructure and resources, produces unconventional performance.[50]

Country	Gold Medals Per Capita
Bahamas	27.87
Hungary	18.74
Finland	18.23
Sweden	14.65
New Zealand	11.20
Norway	11.07
East Germany	9.50
Jamaica	**8.78**
Denmark	8.29
Bulgaria	7.77
Estonia	7.54
Cuba	7.50
Australia	6.55
Switzerland	6.12
Netherlands	5.54
Romania	4.68
Great Britain	4.20
Slovenia	3.85
Belgium	3.71
Italy	3.57
Croatia	3.41
France	3.40
Greece	3.36
United States	3.21
Czechoslovakia	3.14

50 Aaron O'Neill, "Average Number of Medals Won Per Capita at the Summer Olympics from 1896 to 2020 (per One Million Inhabitants)," Statista, June 21, 2022, https://www.statista.com/statistics/1102056/summer-olympics-average-medals-per-capita-since-1892/.

It's unclear why a tiny country such as Jamaica produces such disproportionate performances. Some believe that Champs and the extensive high school rigor necessary to succeed there are the major reasons for Jamaica's dominance. Others believe that track is woven into Jamaican culture. There are even those in the sports scientific community who suggest that Jamaicans are genetically predisposed for success in short-distance sprints. Or maybe it's this:

Jamaicans believe that "wi likkle but wi tallawah." This colloquialism, written in Jamaican patois, translates to "we are small, but we are tall." This is a reaction to a slight or a perceived slight. In this case, that perceived slight is being a small island underdog, and many inhabitants believe Jamaica doesn't get the credit it deserves. Declaring "we are tall" is announcing to the world that, as a nation, they are mighty.

This is the patriotic version of Barry O'Shea. A nation of people amalgamated around a perceived slight is both unifying and inspiring. Jamaica has immense pride in its independence. A nation that, through extensive resistance, abolished slavery thirty years before their American counterparts. A country steeped in culture and tradition. A nation that is only one-tenth the geographic size of New York City and has a population of less than one percent of the entire United States yet still believes they are tall.

And so is Usain St. Leo Bolt!

CHAPTER 11

MAJORITY RULES RULE

> *Whenever you find yourself on the side of the majority, it is time to pause and reflect.*
>
> —Mark Twain

Paradoxes are problematic because they're retrospective. By the time we know we're in the middle of one, we're already in the middle of one. Recognizing them starts with gathering information about the information we don't have. The first step in learning more about a paradox is learning that we need to learn more. And learning more starts with understanding how conventions are created.

Mathematics and science are beautiful ways to determine how the world works. Both are predictable, repeatable, and consistent. Scientific outcomes can be obtained by following the scientific method. Data can be shared, and similar outcomes can be reproduced elsewhere. Mathematics is similar. Equations are consistent and have predictable outcomes when all the same variables are used. Unfortunately, science and mathematics don't always account for the most variable of all variables—human beings.

Paradoxes are created when we falsely believe humans will follow hard and fast rules. Usain Bolt confounded track science with new variables that hadn't previously been accounted for. That mathematical conundrum doesn't just happen in track and field. For most human endeavors, we will never account for all the variables. We often fall into the trap of assuming that our beliefs are as infallible as mathematics. Paradoxes develop because of confidence or, rather, overconfidence. Even in the face of evidence to the contrary, our instinct is to protect what we've always known.

The *Journal of Sports Science and Medicine* was confident in their analysis that the maximum height of successful sprinters was several inches shorter than the fastest sprinter in history. How did they get it wrong? They used science. They used mathematics. So how did they create a convention and publish their findings with the utmost confidence?

It isn't anyone's fault. This happens all the time. Human beings create this confidence by using consensus. Groupthink is a form of consensus. Basketball recruiting is a form of consensus. When people make decisions or recommendations, they use what is collectively known to create standards. They also use what is collectively unknown to create those same standards. Standards then are filled with both knowns and unknowns.

When a group of experts get into a room to develop a standard, how do they create consensus among so many people? For the most part, the process of creating a consensus is organic. More often than not, it takes on a life of its own. Like a viral social media post, consensus usually develops in an unconstructed way.

CHAPTER 11

Thousands of coaches and scouts didn't get together and vote on Steph Curry's college and NBA potential. It just sort of happened. One person writes an evaluation, and the other signs off on it. One person comments, and the other silently nods. One person makes an assertion, and the other disagrees but refuses to be disagreeable.

When scientists publish their conclusions, peers scurry to prove or disprove those findings. As much as we'd like it to be, greatness isn't science. When identifying potential greatness, we don't always follow the scientists' urge to reproduce the data. If someone who is well respected makes an assessment, it's mostly accepted whether it's validated or not.

Other than a few who took the time to disprove the Rivals.com hypothesis, Stephen Curry's scouting report was accepted as truth. The idea that he wasn't athletic enough and shot too many bad shots went viral. Even worse, almost every industry expert echoed the sentiment without having seen him play. They accepted the other scientists' conclusions without attempting to reproduce the experiment themselves. Now that's bad science!

We see this all the time. We ascribe certain qualities to groups of people based on our preconceived notions, without taking the time to assess them individually. In some cases those premature and often stereotypical assessments can be a minor annoyance. In other cases those assessments can be downright fatal.

Making assumptions about a particular person's qualities based on the color of their skin, heritage, or gender is almost universally unacceptable. But when it comes to picking winners and losers, we do it without batting an eye. These assumptions cloud our ability to accurately evaluate people and their ability to succeed. Unfortunately, they can "go viral" before we know it. Fortunately, our society has more structured ways of building consensus.

America's foundation was built on another kind of shared consensus—democracy. Dr. Martin Luther King Jr. became a hero by fighting to ensure everyone had equal opportunity. He believed that race, color, or creed should never be a reason not to have a voice. He believed in this principle so profoundly that he was willing to die to ensure every American was granted equal opportunity.

In America's representative democracy, having a say is directly proportional to having a vote. Dr. Martin Luther King Jr. ultimately lost his life defending those who couldn't defend themselves, but he didn't lose the fight. Things aren't perfect, and the United States still isn't fully united. But without Dr. King, many African Americans wouldn't have the voice they have today.

As a political framework, many would argue that democracy is at the top of the heap. As long as you don't run around and hurt people, freedom is what every society strives for. Having the ability to have a say in the country you live in is one of those feel-good things. Not only is it fair, but it also allows everyone in society to influence the laws and rules that govern them.

Unlike groupthink or erroneous assessments that go viral, voting seems like a logical method to give everyone a say. Instead of a consensus, it creates a majority. One would assume that creating a majority is a much fairer and more reproducible way of identifying greatness. But that's far from the case.

The majority of scouts and coaches didn't think that Steph Curry would be successful. A vote wouldn't change anything about that fact. Instead of a blindly wrong and erroneous consensus, it would have been a wrong and erroneous majority vote. In fact, every year a group of voters comes together to vote for the best high school basketball players in the country. Each high school athlete they select gets an opportunity to play in the McDonald's All-American Game. Selection for this honor is the pinnacle of an athlete's high school career. Of course, Stephen Curry wasn't chosen. By consensus and by majority, he remained underrated.

If track coaches in Jamaica and around the globe voted on whether a six-foot-five sprinter would dominate the one-hundred-meter for three straight Olympics, they would have voted incorrectly. Majorities don't work! Dr. Martin Luther King Jr. was fighting for African Americans to have the right to have their vote counted after African Americans already had the right to have their vote counted. Almost one hundred years after the Fifteenth Amendment, African Americans were still fighting to have a voice in a country where everyone was supposed to have a voice. How does that happen? That happened because majorities are just that. They're majorities!

Majorities work when most people want something similar. When the majority of people want the same things and vote the same way, the majority of them will feel like their voice is heard. And the minority? The minority can't change the rules and laws of a country by themselves.

Bob McKillop can't change college basketball recruiting by himself. Although his disruption changed Steph Curry's course, he wasn't able to change the course of others. Majorities are great for *majorities*. For them, democracy becomes religion. Unfortunately, if you aren't a part of the majority, your voice will always be muted—even with an equal vote.

Democracies are great when everyone wants the same thing, and they might even be great when there are two evenly matched factions. But majorities are horrible for the less than one percent, who, by definition, are outliers. I love what Dr. King did for America, but history sometimes confuses his real contribution. Dr. King wasn't fighting to increase the impact of the votes from the minority. He was hoping to change the hearts, minds, and ways of thinking of the majority. That was his greatness. On a much smaller scale, I am trying to do the same.

I hope to change how we build consensus and how we vote for those we believe will be successful. I hope that whenever you find yourself on the side of the majority, you take a moment to pause and reflect. This doesn't mean democracies aren't the best way to run countries or organizations. It just means that democracies aren't the best way to identify greatness.

In our exuberance to find the next Curry or Bolt, we forget the nonstandard process that created each of them. We try to create standards for nonstandard individuals. We try to analyze less-than-one-percenters and create consensus when we really should be looking for the next less-than-one-percenters, who, by definition, will disrupt that recently created consensus.

Stephen Curry is a perfect example. He's the poster child for the new NBA. The three-pointer, a shot that Curry elevated to new heights, changed the way NBA coaches and NBA executives manage their teams. If we look at three-point attempts per game in the NBA over time, we see that the number has gone up year after year. The number of three-point attempts was pretty stable until the 2009–2010 season. Three-point attempts have increased almost every year since then. Fifteen years later, the number of three-pointers attempted per game almost doubled. Something changed during the 2009–2010 NBA basketball season. Is it merely a coincidence that it was Steph's rookie season?[51]

---

51 "NBA League Averages—per Game," Basketball Reference, accessed June 21, 2024, https://www.basketball-reference.com/leagues/NBA_stats_per_game.html.

CHAPTER 11

Rank	NBA Season	Three-Point Attempts
1	2021-2022	35.2
2	2020-2021	34.6
3	2019-2020	34.1
4	2018-2019	32.0
5	2017-2018	29.0
6	2016-2017	27.0
7	2015-2016	24.1
8	2014-2015	22.4
9	2013-2014	21.5
10	2012-2013	20.0
11	2011-2012	18.4
12	2008-2009	18.1
13	2007-2008	18.1
14	2009-2010	18.1
15	2010-2011	19.0

The NBA is an intriguing organization. Although many see it as an enterprise or corporation, it functions more like a marketplace. The central office sets the rules by which the independent franchises function. Like other industries, when one company does well in the marketplace, others take notice. More importantly, they try to reproduce that success. It sounds a little like our scientific method, except success in the NBA doesn't always follow science's predictable and reproducible rules. After all, it's a league full of humans.

Although the NBA pits five human beings against five other human beings to see who can score the most points in forty-eight minutes, they try their best to be analytical. To that end, between 2009 and 2012, the NBA increased its reliance on analytics. Franchises embraced this trend, hoping to gain a competitive edge. They focused on two goals: maximizing points scored and increasing the average points per shot.

In an effort to achieve these goals, teams spread the court, played faster, and started shooting more three-pointers. Interestingly, it wasn't just a few outliers that tried to gain this perceived advantage. They all made the change! Every single franchise in the NBA started shooting more threes.

Not only did they all shoot more threes per possession, but they also increased the number of possessions so they could play faster—so they could shoot even *more* threes. It sounded like a less-than-one-percent thing to do. It sounded innovative. It sounded like a Coach McNeil moment. And it likely would've been one of those moments if they hadn't all done it. Every NBA franchise did it. The old NBA became the new NBA, and they all group-thought their way to the same competitive advantage.

In fear of being left behind, every franchise began using the same revolutionary analytic approach. Shoot more threes so you can play faster, so you can shoot more threes, and so on. Do you see the signs? This is a convention! This is a consensus! This is a majority! This isn't a less-than-one-percent moment! This is tantamount to every one-hundred-meter sprinter in the 2009 World Athletics Championships measuring six foot five. If that were the case, the distance per stride

CHAPTER 11

would become irrelevant. If everyone were the same height, then Usain Bolt and Coach McNeil wouldn't be considered revolutionary. You can't be a less-than-one-percenter doing what everybody else is doing.

The "new" NBA group-thought its way to a fast-paced, three-point shooting league that's extremely exciting to watch. But something interesting happened. If you're a general manager, coach, or franchise owner, winning requires building a team of the best three-point shooters. The focus on three-point shooters should've created a league that had better three-point shooting. If all the teams are taking and making more threes, and if all the franchises are building teams with the best three-point shooters, then the NBA's shooting percentage should increase over time.

To find that out, let's analyze the fifteen best three-point shooting years in the NBA. The most accurate year from the three-point line is 1995–1996. That year Dennis Scott was the most prolific three-point shooter with 267 shots. Tim Legler was the most accurate three-point shooter—making over 52 percent! On a point-per-shot basis, the most efficient player that year was 1996 NBA champion Michael Jordan, who didn't focus on shooting threes at all.[52]

---

52   Basketball Reference, "NBA League Averages—per Game."

LESS THAN ONE PERCENT

Rank	NBA Season	Three-Point Attempts
1	1995-96	36.7
2	2008-09	36.7
3	2020-21	36.7
4	2007-08	36.2
5	2017-18	36.2
6	1996-97	36.0
7	2013-14	36.0
8	1994-95	35.9
9	2012-13	35.9
10	2005-06	35.8
11	2006-07	35.8
12	2010-11	35.8
13	2016-17	35.8
14	2019-20	35.8
15	2022-23	35.8

With respect to percentages, the analytic boom didn't result in NBA teams improving their ability to make three-point shots. With all the resources the NBA has, we should expect the top three-point shooting percentages in history during the years that teams adopted this analytic strategy. But because every single NBA franchise decided to play the same way at the same time, they inadvertently nullified that strategy. One franchise stood out for a different reason. The Golden State Warriors had Coach McKillop's former player Stephen Curry. He helped the Golden State Warriors win four of the eight NBA championships between 2015 and 2022.

Shooting threes to play faster so you can shoot more threes isn't as effective as shooting more threes to play faster so you can shoot more threes—*well*. In an era that places a premium on shooting threes, the team that will have the advantage is the team that can make more threes. The player who has made the most threes since 2009 is Stephen Curry. One could argue that 2015 to 2022 were his best years. During that period he was named the NBA's MVP twice. It's no wonder that the Warriors' dominance coincided with Curry's virtuoso performances.

The NBA found itself on the side of the majority, and they didn't pause and reflect. Majority rules but not when you're trying to find greatness. Seeking out and finding greatness is an entirely different endeavor. When everyone is doing the same thing, then everyone is doing the same thing. Greatness is not the same thing.

The new NBA standard is exciting, but all the teams doing the same unconventional thing is still a convention. Standardizing the competitive environment by taking more three-pointers created an advantage for individuals who could make them. Coach McKillop gave Stephen Curry the license to shoot any shot he wanted if he worked on it, and the post-analytic-revolution NBA also gave him that license.

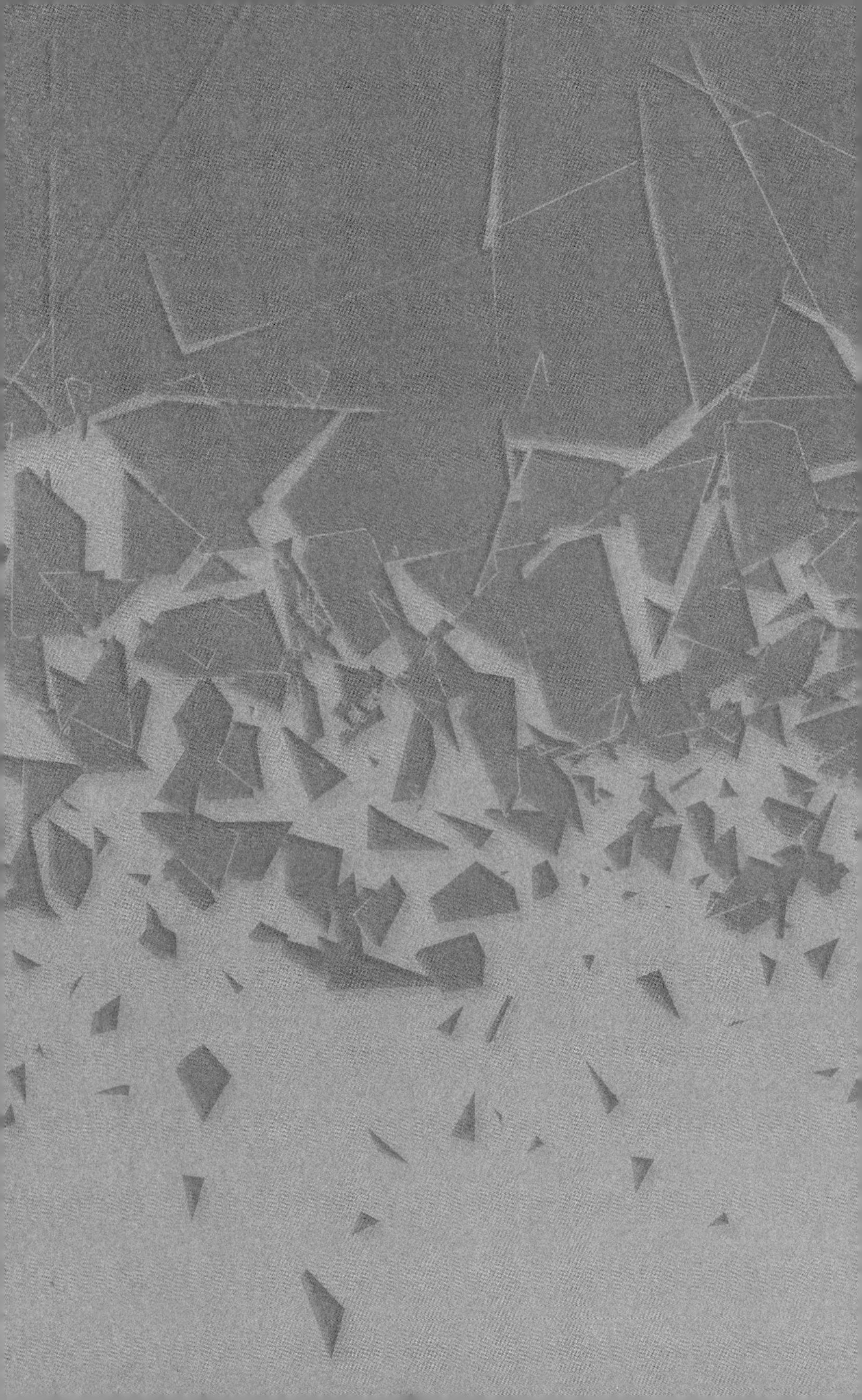

CHAPTER 12

INSOLENCE

> Conformity is the last refuge of the unimaginative.
>
> –Oscar Wilde

Analyzing unconventional world-class sprinters and all-star basketball players is compelling. It isn't as compelling to watch sixth-place contestants compete, but this sport has rules, standards, and traditions. It's a matter of courtesy and procedure. Something miraculous could happen, but most of the time, sixth place is just sixth place. At this point in the competition, this obligatory performance is more for pride than anything else.

These fans aren't like any other spectators. They aren't necessarily watching to see who'll win. They watch to appreciate the technical choreography and nuanced skill that often accompanies these ornate performances—even the ones that seemingly don't matter. Those overly educated fans who sardine themselves into positions to catch a glimpse were on the edge of their seats because even the worst of these competitors were graceful and powerful. Considering their commitment to refining their craft and the years of dedication and training, they more than deserve the crowd's reverence. It's one thing to jump, spin, and land at full speed. It's an entirely different thing to jump, spin, and land at full speed—on ice.

Figure skating has to be one of the most difficult Olympic disciplines. One could argue that it's the signature event of the entire Olympics. Winter Olympic sports are so unique that they have their own special event, alternating every two years with the summer version. The zenith of these competitive efforts, which occur farthest from the sun, is figure skating. Figure skating isn't just a fantastic spectacle. It's also seductively dangerous. Nothing is scarier than skating full speed, planting, jumping, and spinning in the air. I stand corrected. Nothing is scarier than doing all of that and then landing!

Undaunted, she skated to the center of the ice, took her pose, and waited for the muted music to start. She really stood out. She looked more like a gymnast than a figure skater. Her loud light blue and gold suit told its story through each sequin's shimmering reflection of the ice. Long, dangling earrings and a chain with a pendant at the back completed her distracting ensemble, which the judges duly noted.

The routine started with a signature figure skating spin that started slowly and accelerated as the skater tightened her frame. Then she rocketed into the air, spinning three times before her delayed landing. It was breathtaking! At the same time, it was dismissively nonchalant.

She pivoted and skated backward while developing even more speed. She jumped a second time and nailed the landing. Right after she landed, she bounced into another jump. She attempted three

CHAPTER 12

more dizzying levitating spins several feet above the ice but overspun and fell. Using her arm to brace the fall, she confidently popped right back up. Mistakes aren't supposed to make skaters more confident, but this was no ordinary skater.

Figure skating outcomes are a bit of a black box, but that fall almost assuredly hurt her chances. At least by her demeanor, there was no indication of her folly. She got up as gracefully as ever and continued. She picked up speed again and landed a perfect triple salchow—a move invented by Ulrich Salchow in 1909 in which the skater takes off from the inside of one foot and lands on the outside of the other. It was brilliantly done! The crowd, who had become accustomed to their collective forced intimacy, showered her with applause.

The routine that she was doing was part of her free skate. This is one portion of a more comprehensive skating program when skaters, within technical confines, get to show their stuff. It lasts for a total of four minutes and has several technical criteria that must be included. She continued to land many exceedingly difficult jumps and interspersed what appeared to be choreographed elegant moves.

From the way she bounded on the ice, it was impossible to tell that this was her last of two segments for the day. She looked like a cross between a ballet dancer and a professional basketball dunk contestant. Then the music changed abruptly. Serene and inspiring was replaced with piercing staccato. And her body language and demeanor embodied that change.

"She has great expression.… But her problems artistically are the breaks in the choreography before she does her jumps.… The judges don't like that. They want you to flow into the next element," Scott Hamilton, a figure skating hero in his own right, commented as he was calling the competition for the CBS television broadcast.

Another jump landed perfectly. She was picking up momentum. The music matched her defiant demeanor, as if the fall only two minutes earlier happened in some alternative reality. Another jump—perfect! With even more speed than before, she again skated backward, and that was when it happened.

"Backflip! Totally illegal in competition. She's doing this to get the crowd. She's gonna get nailed—ha ha!" Scott Hamilton almost screamed. He was both amazed, enthused, and utterly nervous. He wasn't necessarily nervous for himself. He was nervous for her.

"You could hear the gasps from the knowledgeable crowd. That's an in-your-face move." Verne Lundquist, who teamed up with Scott Hamilton to bring the Olympic story to the American audience, jumped in.

She was in her element. Despite the eruption of energy, her movements were even more precise. She finished with a series of spins and a huge smile. She was glowing. The music and her spin both synchronously slowed.

"The reaction from this judging panel will be really interesting," Lundquist told viewers in both shock and supportive disapproval. "And she finishes her program with her back to the judges!"

She finished to a raucous ovation. The crowd was awed by both the performance and her insolence. Already in sixth place and likely to sink even lower, she was the star of the day. After that performance she wasn't going anywhere near the podium, and that was fine. She wasn't a fan of the podium anyway.

Her name was Surya Varuna Claudine Bonaly.

The judges, six women and three men, were unenthused. In fact, they were downright incensed. They didn't share the crowd's jubilation over what could've been one of the most impressive feats in figure skating history. One of the judges painfully pressed her left hand

CHAPTER 12

to her face. Two fingers at her temple and her thumb dug into her wrinkled cheek as she fervently wrote on her score sheet. Her expression was that of a disapproving teacher grading a failing paper from a future valedictorian. She appeared to be using her hand to hide from a crowd that was still partially standing in ovation.

Another judge in a purple overcoat with a button-down purple shirt and bright red hair hovered over her work. She was writing intensely but took a moment to peer over her glasses at the ice. The glasses hung precariously from the end of her long, pointed nose—the way the principal glares at delinquent students in detention. Two other judges started an animated conversation. They looked like two parents arguing over their fifth grader's report card, whose Harvard acceptance was in early jeopardy.

"There is the panel of nine. I don't sense any looks of approval," said Lundquist.

But even as the next contestant took the ice, the applause continued. Bonaly repeatedly curtsied in acknowledgment of their cheers.

"Well, obviously, she doesn't care about the marks because she's not going to get 'em for this," Hamilton said, partly admonishing and mostly admiring. "Layout position, one-foot landing. She's the only one in the world who can do that. She's so strong."

And the scores from those judges? They were horrible. After her once-in-a-lifetime performance, she dropped from a mediocre sixth place to an uncomplimentary tenth place. The judges had spoken. Surya's disruptive move was unconventional and nonstandard. It was also illegal.

Not many tenth-place performances bring an entire rink to their feet. Not many tenth-place performances bring the entire rink to their feet *and* thoroughly incense the judges. Why did someone who performed a maneuver that had never been done in history score so poorly?

This is the Bonaly paradox.

Although the system has been revamped multiple times since the 1998 Nagano Olympics, figure skating is scored by convention and consensus. At that time judges evaluated each skater by a subjective set of strict rules. Take a moment to read that again. Judges evaluated each skater by a subjective set of strict rules. That should make your head hurt.

The *Oxford Dictionary* defines subjective as "an evaluation based on or influenced by personal feelings, tastes, or opinions." Therefore, judges have collectively created rules based on personal feelings, tastes, and opinions. How could the judges possibly create something objective while filtering through the distorting lens of subjectivity? Even if that were possible, whose subjectivity would be the standard? Who made these rules? In the case of skating, the International Skating Union (ISU) made the rules.

If you go to the ISU's website, you'll find this:[53]

> The International Skating Union, founded in 1892, is the exclusive international sport federation recognized by the International Olympic Committee (IOC) administering sports in the branches of Figure Skating and Speed Skating throughout the world.... The objectives of the ISU are to regulate, govern and promote the sports in the Figure Skating and Speed Skating Branches and their organized development on the basis of friendship and mutual understanding between sportsmen and women. The ISU works to broaden interest in all its disciplines by increasing their popular-

---

53 *Constitution and General Regulations 2022*, International Skating Union, June 2022, https://www.isu.org/inside-isu/rules-regulations/isu-statutes-constitution-regulations-technical/29326-constitution-general-regulations-2022/file.

CHAPTER 12

ity, improving their quality, and increasing the number of participants throughout the world.

They continue,

The ISU Council is the highest ISU body between Congresses and its main functions are to determine the policies of the ISU and decide upon the general coordination of the ISU structure, allot ISU Championships and other ISU Events, checking that the accounting for and management of assets are subject to adequate controls, the preparation and submission to Congress of annual budgets, decisions regarding the admission or suspension of Members, decisions on appeals from the decisions of the Technical Committees and ISU Officials involving violation of technical sport Rules amongst many others.

The ISU's objective, by its own admission, is to regulate and govern. They create rules for the sport of figure skating based on friendship and mutual understanding. Its primary function is to determine the policies of the ISU and decide upon the general coordination of the ISU structure. This is a convention!

The idea that the backflip should be illegal wasn't determined by patient scientific study or repeating repeatable experiments. The idea that the backflip should be illegal was a consensus. To that end, the ISU painstakingly outlined that no skater shall ever do a flip and land on two feet. That "rule" limited the creativity of figure skaters. Becoming a great figure skater required adherence to the ISU-accepted practice. Those who failed to stay in that box paid the price.

LESS THAN ONE PERCENT

And the judges? Well, they judged. Before we judge the judges too harshly, they shouldn't get all the blame. They were simply supporting the convention, an unfortunate and unintended side effect of the skating world's collective groupthink. It didn't matter that the crowd was paralyzed in amazement and awe. Skaters who want to win are compelled to play by the rules.

Figure skating wasn't looking for greatness. It was looking for how closely an individual's performance adhered to a particular methodology—a methodology that was created to maintain that convention. It's completely circular logic. Adhere to the standard created by a convention so that the convention can continue to create a standard. In other words judges are responsible for maintaining skating standards by rewarding those who perform closest to those standards. Unfortunately for Surya, greatness wasn't standard.

At the time Surya was the only figure skater to ever land a backflip on one leg. In doing so, she disrupted a convention that ultimately threatened the ISU standard. It wouldn't be fair to accept Surya Bonaly's backflip. That would give her an unfair advantage, mainly because other skaters didn't have the skill or athleticism to accomplish such a feat. What the ISU deemed "dangerous" wasn't dangerous for Surya at all.

In all her years touring with Champions on Ice, the professional show she signed onto after Nagano, she never missed the backflip. Never! Her backflip in Nagano was the first time she performed a backflip in a competition, but it wasn't the first time she landed one. Her first backflip was at twelve years old. Twelve years old! Backflipping may have been dangerous for everyone else, but it was automatic for Surya.

The backflip—called a "somersault" by the ISU—was banned after American Terry Kubicka backflipped at the 1976 Winter Olympics.

CHAPTER 12

The ISU never issued an official explanation for the backflip ban. The ISU adopted a position that a somersault was an improper skating maneuver because skating elements weren't allowed to land on two feet. At some level, this seems reasonable. All sports have rules in place to protect their athletes. However, if you dig deeper into ISU's 155-page *Special Regulations and Technical Rules,* you'll find the ISU is protecting the ISU.

Even the music skaters use during their programs is standardized: "All Competitors shall furnish competition music of excellent quality in a format and means announced in the announcement of the competition in accordance with Rule 112."[54] What in the world is music of excellent quality anyway? What is the measure of excellent quality? Is it opera or classical or jazz or country? Judges evaluate routines based on a figure skater's technical skills, artistic approach—whatever that is—and choice of music.

In their defense the ISU is creating standards by which all skaters can be fairly evaluated. Standardization isn't altogether a terrible thing, but the challenge with standardization is it levels the playing field. This creates an environment where judges aren't looking for the best skater; they're looking for the skater who best represents the standard.

It's tantamount to a race where every runner is the same height, every team uses analytics to shoot more three-point shots, or emergency patients are seen one after the other. Setting a standard and measuring how one's performance conforms to that standard isn't the same thing as recognizing greatness. And that was the challenge with Surya Bonaly. She was nonstandard *and* great—a combination that didn't mix well with the figure skating convention.

Surya's blank expression as she heard her scores was unexpected. As they announced the scores that made it obvious that "she got

---

54   International Skating Union, *Constitution and General Regulations 2022.*

95

nailed," why didn't Surya have a more boisterous reaction? As Surya and her mother listened to the scores, they had the same expression as they silently talked to each other—somewhere between a wry smile and an irreverent blank stare. Her mother, who was also her coach and made her costumes, looked at her adoringly, raised both eyebrows, and kissed her on the cheek.

Surya didn't react like an individual who had made history in competition, nor did she react like an individual who made history and got docked for it. Their reactions to this devastating judging miscalculation made it seem like they expected those scores. They weren't surprised at all!

When it came to judges, Surya was no stranger to the oddity of their verdicts. This wasn't the first time the judges had been at odds with the crowd. In 1994 Bonaly suffered what she believed was a similar injustice. During the World Championships that year, Surya was so disappointed with the judges and her scores that she refused to stand on the podium next to Yuka Sato.

ISU representative Olaf Paulsen approached her and urged her to take the place on the podium. As he implored her to comply, Surya was violently booed by the crowd. She silently refused. Paulsen shook his head and placed the medal around her neck. He shook her hand and forcibly moved her onto the podium. She stepped up to avoid falling. They exchanged a long awkward handshake, and he continued to encourage her. Visibly sobbing, she removed the medal from around her neck, and the crowd reflexively moaned. Still crying, she bunched up the medal in her right fist.

Surya Bonaly lost to Yuka Sato by the slimmest of margins, even though Sato had fallen during one of her jumps. Bonaly lost points on her presentation and artistic flare—a distinction that wasn't entirely clear to those who watched. Bonaly's jumps were athletic and technically sound. Yuka's jumps were simple and elegant. Yuka was an artist, and Bonaly was an athlete. The judges chose artistry in adherence to the ISU convention.

The second-place finish hurt, but it likely hurt a bit more because the same thing had happened the previous year. This was Surya's second straight silver! She lost to gold medalist Oksana Baiul by almost the same slimmest of margins in 1993. On the surface, Bonaly could be criticized for her behavior on the podium. However, looking more closely and considering the reaction to her backflip several years later, it's easier to understand her dismay.

This was Surya's Barry O'Shea. Losing once was bad enough, but losing twice by almost the same margin was a slight that she couldn't let go. Surya's Achilles' heel was her presentation, and her scores often reflected that. In a field where the music had to be of sufficient quality, it isn't surprising that "presentation" had become a convention. Something as subjective as presentation is prone to groupthink and open to subjective consensus. Surya's reaction on the podium might have seemed extreme. But at its root, her response was the defiant embodiment of Jamaica's "wi likkle but wi tallawah."

Unfortunately for Surya, the judges were correct. Sato conformed to the ISU's arbitrary scoring convention, and Surya didn't. And while Surya was appropriately enraged at the judges, she should have been even more outraged at figure skating. She wasn't what figure skating was looking for. She was unconventional in so many ways.

For a skater, Surya's upbringing was typical. Her mother, a well-established skating coach, put her on the ice as early as two. Surya was immersed in skating's most intricate details while she watched her mother train other skaters. Skating wasn't her only discipline; Surya participated in many sports. Most notably, she was a phenomenal gymnast. That gymnast foundation and her incredible athleticism made her approach to figure skating unique. It isn't that Surya wasn't technically sound; her tumbling experience made jumps effortless. But the skating establishment preferred elegance over athleticism.

Surya's jumping ability meant that she could push the envelope even further. The ISU made an appropriate assumption that backflips were too dangerous, and they were right. Backflips were too dangerous for skaters not named Surya Bonaly. One critical component of the backflip ban was the rule that figure skating jumps should always land on one foot. Before Nagano, those who attempted backflips landed on two feet. Thus, by that definition, it was illegal. So Bonaly legally landed her backflip on one foot.

Sonja Kaminski, a longtime United States figure skating judge, described Bonaly's predicament in an email highlighted in a February 2018 Andscape article.[55]

> Coming from a competitive gymnastics background, she had an unorthodox jumping and technical style, which, at the time, was not in line with the traditional style of skating that was expected and accepted by the broader skating community. That time in skating was the "age of elegance," and both Surya and Tonya [Harding] displayed athleticism, not finesse.

Surya Bonaly's athleticism was an advantage that thumbed its proverbial nose at figure skating conventions. Instead of changing the convention to allow elements that can be done by more athletic skaters, the ISU indirectly penalized more athletic skaters. What the ISU did to Surya Bonaly would be like the International Association

---

55   Eryn Mathewson, "Former Olympian Surya Bonaly Says Don't Call Her a Rebel, Call Her Fearless," Andscape, February 22, 2018, https://andscape.com/features/former-olympian-surya-bonaly-says-dont-call-her-a-rebel-call-her-fearless/.

of Athletics Federations banning Usain Bolt because he was too tall or like the NBA banning Stephen Curry because he made shots from too far away from the basket.

Unless they're checked by disruptors such as Surya, conventions and their subsequent paradoxes persist. Surya's Barry O'Shea moment compelled her to challenge the skating establishment. Maybe appropriately so, she believed the world she loved rejected her. That 1994 World Championship rejection culminated in her history making defiance.

Surya didn't feel like she fit in, so she decided not to. While skating didn't accept who she was, that backflip was her declaration that she was no longer looking for skating's approval. While the crowd, commentators, and contestants knew who really won, the judges group-thought themselves to a different answer.

The Surya Bonaly paradox lifted the veil on what was an unfair, biased, and corrupt institution. This disruption highlighted the difficulty of creating objective standards with subjective and often erroneous conventions. Just like emergency medical care changed forever after RME, the Bonaly paradox changed the skating fabric.

That fabric finally began to tear in the 2002 Winter Olympic Games, when two judges were accused of fixing an outcome. A pair of Russian skaters were awarded the gold medal, even though the Canadian pair had clearly outperformed them. The result was so obviously biased that the ISU immediately suspended both judges—one of whom was the head of the French skating federation.

Bias and corruption forced the ISU to completely revamp the scoring system to become more objective. They changed figure skating's scoring system to emphasize technical skill and athletic prowess rather than subjective criteria. Unfortunately for Surya, skating's sweeping change came over a decade too late.

Surya Bonaly didn't win skating's most coveted prize, but her tenth-place finish changed skating irrevocably. Her lack of conformity and disdain for skating's conventions should be applauded and not booed. The courage to land a backflip at the Olympics came from her need to disrupt the skating standard—a standard that didn't account for a former gymnast, überathletic daughter of a skating coach who deemed second place intolerable.

Surya shared her feelings in a February 16, 2022, *Time* magazine article.[56]

> I did not have the idea of being the first woman to do a quad.... It was, "Hey, I can do triples so now what's next?" When you know how to do some elements, you always try to raise the bar and do something different, and not stick to the same things forever. I thought it would be good for me, because I was also very athletic, I could just try and work on [quad jumps].

French judge Anne Hardy-Thomas, who was one of the competition judges for Bonaly's backflip, responded to an Olympic delegate who described Bonaly as insolent during a postperformance interview: "She did well for all the past years."[57]

---

56 Alice Park,"Quadruple Jumps Are Transforming Women's Figure Skating. Surya Bonaly Tried to Do It 30 Years Ago," *Time*, February 16, 2022, https://time.com/6143521/quadruple-jump-figure-skating-surya-bonaly/.

57 Binge Audio, "Surya Bonaly, Corps et Lames: Episode 6," retrieved May 19, 2020.

CHAPTER 13

TO MORROW'S LAST CHANCE

> *There comes a point when, tired of losing, you decide to stop failing yourself, or at least to try, or to send up the final flare, one last chance.*
>
> —Colum McCann

It's one thing to make mistakes about who will and won't succeed, but it's an entirely different and more disastrous thing when we make mistakes about who will fail. The space between average and above average isn't nearly as vast as the chasm between average and failure. Paradoxes may limit the ascension of a few to superstar status, such as Curry and Bolt. But many more paradoxes leave entire portions of our society behind.

Based on gross domestic product (GDP), which represents the total monetary or market value of goods and services produced by a country, the United States of America is one of the wealthiest countries in the world.[58] If this wealth were divided equally among all Americans, many of the demographic disparities that exist ... wouldn't.

Although the poorest Americans earn more than the poorest worldwide,[59] it's a travesty that many Americans don't have the same access to America's greatness. If you look at the average American household income by racial demographic, you'll see a stark difference in the distribution of that GDP.[60]

Race/Ethnicity	Average Household Income	Median Income	Top 1% Income
White Non-Hispanic	$75,132.80	$52,011.00	$460,175.00
Black	$51,394.59	$38,800.00	$250,001.00
American Indian	$49,159.31	$35,000.00	$400,000.00
Asian	$83,154.31	$60,000.00	$461,750.00
Pacific Islander	$58,684.18	$42,800.00	$351,025.00
Two or More Races	$50,589.88	$35,101.00	$280,203.00
Hispanic	$45,612.64	$34,153.00	$240,012.00

---

58 Aaron O'Neill, "The 20 Countries with the Largest Gross Domestic Product (GDP) in 2024," Statista, June 25, 2024, https://www.statista.com/statistics/268173/countries-with-the-largest-gross-domestic-product-gdp/.

59 Robert M. Whaples, "Where Do the Poorest Americans Stand in the Income Distribution among All People Ever Born?" *The Independent Review* 27, no. 1 (Summer 2022), https://www.independent.org/publications/tir/article.asp?id=1744.

60 PK, "Income by Race: Average, Top One Percent, Median, and Inequalities," DQYDJ, accessed June 21, 2024, https://dqydj.com/income-by-race/.

CHAPTER 13

The difference, for example, between Black Americans and White Americans in average household income is around $24,000. A child born into a White American family then has access to approximately 32 percent more income than a child born into a Black family. The entire household feels the impact of that disparity, but it's likely even more detrimental to the most vulnerable—the children.

Logically, children born into households with more income have access to more resources. Whether it's math tutoring or piano lessons, kids with access to more resources have a distinct advantage. This isn't to say that children from poorer households can't succeed, but a lack of resources makes succeeding that much harder.

And that's just the beginning. As incomes continue to rise, the differential between those two groups widens. If we look at the top 1 percent of American earners, the gap between Black and White Americans has grown exponentially to approximately $210,000. Children born into the wealthiest White American households have access to nearly the same income as *two* Black American families combined.

When we scrutinize the data, the relationship between African Americans and wealth—relative to other demographic subsets in America—is shocking. And if reading about it is shocking, could you imagine being ten years old and dreaming about the American Dream? While even the most astute ten-year-olds don't necessarily know the data, they more than know the experience. And what they experience likely manifests itself in what they aspire to achieve.

The Association of American Medical Colleges reports that about 14 percent of active physicians in the United States are African American.[61] According to Zippia, a company that collects career

---

61 "Diversity in Medicine: Facts and Figures 2019," Association of American Medical Colleges, accessed June 21, 2024, https://www.aamc.org/data-reports/workforce/data/figure-18-percentage-all-active-physicians-race/ethnicity-2018.

demographic data, of the almost two hundred thousand actively employed engineers in the United States, only about 3 percent are African American.[62] Whereas the NBA, a league that is 70 percent African American, has a per-player average income of $9.7 million.[63] Players in the NFL, which is almost 60 percent African American, earn an average income of about $3.3 million.[64]

Considering the data from the NBA, NFL, physicians, and engineers, ambitious African American ten-year-olds looking for a role model are more likely to find that role model in athletics. Astute ten-year-olds are unconsciously convinced that success is more likely as an athlete and less likely as a physician or engineer. It isn't just ten-year-olds. Often, their parents inadvertently assume the same thing.

Youth sports has become a $15 billion industry.[65] Where does most of the revenue come from? It comes from parents! Sports participation is an opportunity for families to spend time together and for kids to learn life lessons. That said, many parents believe that investing in their child's sport can lead to a scholarship. Colleges around the country offer scholarships for the best athletes. As the cost of college skyrockets, a basketball scholarship could give a child the academic opportunity of a lifetime.

Malcolm Gladwell's book *Outliers* popularized the ten thousand hours philosophy, a concept that describes the time necessary to master a skill. Through meaningful work, success is possible for those

---

62 "Engineer Demographics and Statistics in the US," Zippia, accessed June 21, 2024, https://www.zippia.com/engineer-jobs/demographics/.

63 "Share of Players in the NBA from 2010 to 2023, by Ethnicity," Statista, October 9, 2023, https://www.statista.com/statistics/1167867/nba-players-ethnicity/.

64 Michael Shearer, "What Is the Average and Median NBA Salary for 2023–24 by Position?" Fansided, October 2, 2023, https://fansided.com/posts/what-is-the-average-and-median-nba-salary-for-2023-24-by-position-01hbrqp8mv6f.

65 Sean Gregory, "How Kids' Sports Became a $15 Billion Industry," *Time*, August 24, 2017, https://time.com/4913687/how-kids-sports-became-15-billion-industry/.

CHAPTER 13

who put the time in. As parents of aspiring athletes know, arriving at ten thousand hours in basketball, soccer, or any sport requires money. Coaches and trainers and leagues—all things that can help an athlete get to the requisite ten thousand hours—cost money and a lot of it.

Parents who embark upon their child's basketball journey can spend as much as $5,000 a year. Yes! And that's not even the worst of it. Youth volleyball and youth soccer can cost as much as $6,000![66] The commitment required for this level of athletic pursuit is outstanding. If parents commit to their child's particular athletic discipline as they would commit to piano or chess, that's commendable. But if parents commit to the child's particular athletic discipline because they're investing to increase their chances of an athletic scholarship, they may be misguided.

As an investment tool, $6,000 a year for a potential scholarship isn't exactly a high-yield investment. In 2022 there were 910,804 high school basketball players; of those, 10,601 men and women went on to play Division I college basketball—the highest level of collegiate basketball at which schools award the most and highest financial scholarships.[67] A Division I athletic scholarship covers all tuition, fees, meals, books, room, and board. While the reward is high, a prospective high school basketball player has only a 1.2 percent chance of playing for a Division I basketball program.

So let's check the math. A total of $6,000 a year is the entry investment for a 1.2 percent chance of making about $140,000, the average cost of tuition, room, and board in college. If the goal of this

---

66   Jason Smith, "Paying to Play: How Much Do Club Sports Cost?" *USA Today High School Sports*, August 1, 2017, https://usatodayhss.com/2017/paying-to-play-how-much-do-club-sports-cost.

67   "NCAA Sports Sponsorship and Participation Rates Report," NCAA, updated September 29, 2023, https://ncaaorg.s3.amazonaws.com/research/sportpart/2023RES_SportsSponsorshipParticipationRatesReport.pdf.

investment is to afford college, there are far better financial tools for parents to invest in. A $6,000 annual investment, with a compounded 7 percent interest rate, yields $220,000. That's enough to cover tuition, room and board, a car, and a computer—and still have a little left over.

What about those who can't afford that level of investment? In the 2020–2021 academic school year, the United States government awarded $138.6 billion in student grants.[68] Private colleges awarded students an additional $7.4 billion, of which $100 million went unclaimed.[69] By contrast, the National Collegiate Athletic Association awarded $3.5 billion in athletic scholarships.[70] Can you see it? The paradox here is the belief that athletics is the best way—and presumed, in some cases, to be the only way—to get a college education paid for.

Our society, for better or worse, is still preoccupied with gladiators. Each of those student gladiators is honored on National Signing Day—a day dedicated to the few athletes lucky enough to receive an athletic scholarship. This is a wonderful opportunity to honor those who have dedicated their ten thousand hours and achieved mastery in their athletic craft. Unfortunately, National Signing Day has no academic equivalent. There are no press conferences or media blitzes for students who have dedicated their lives to perfecting their *academic* craft.

In the summer, the most active travel basketball season, parents cram into overcrowded venues where hundreds of people huddle around the courts. Warehouses are turned into massive, minimally

---

[68] Jennifer Ma and Matea Pender, "Trends in College Pricing and Student Aid 2021," College Board, October 2021, https://research.collegeboard.org/media/pdf/trends-college-pricing-student-aid-2021.pdf.

[69] Imed Bouchrika, "72 Scholarship Statistics: 2024 Data, Facts & Analysis," Research.com, June 11, 2024, https://research.com/research/scholarship-statistics.

[70] "Overview," National Collegiate Athletic Association, accessed June 25, 2024, https://www.ncaa.org/sports/2021/2/16/overview.aspx.

CHAPTER 13

air-conditioned gyms—some with as many as twenty claustrophobic courts. Parents pay for their child to play on a team, and they also have to pay for parking, gym, and hotel fees. These aspiring athletes will play five games in four days, hoping to play well enough to garner a scholarship. This type of youth basketball experience, dubbed AAU for Amateur Athletic Union, is where future stars are made.

Not all tournaments have the AAU moniker, but historically, the AAU was the sanctioning body for many youth events. Since then, the youth sports world has exploded. Even with multiple sponsors, shoe company circuits, and sanctioning bodies, the AAU title stuck—the same way we use Kleenex instead of facial tissue.

The best word to describe this environment is fevered. Boys, girls, and their doting parents shuffle from court to crowded court to compete. Some are there to have fun, some are there to improve, some are there for college exposure, but most are there to win. It's hard to believe that winning is that important to ten-year-olds. One look at the parents and the coaches, and you quickly find out that everything of value in the world is riding on the shoulders of these ten-year-old gladiators.

Basketball can be a beautiful game. It's a coordinated symphony of movement and timing. These young athletes are learning about teamwork, sportsmanship, and passion. They're learning life lessons about what it takes to be a part of a team. Unfortunately, they're also learning about the darker side of intense competition.

There are several things you can count on in this highly competitive environment. You can always count on a parent screaming at their kid—a kid who would rather be doing just about anything else. You can always count on a coach berating the refs who always make the wrong call. You can always count on a few older kids playing down a grade to give their team an adolescent and illegal advantage. And you can always count on seeing a kid who is unbelievably talented.

I know a little about AAU basketball because I was an AAU basketball coach and parent. I've spent long hours in hot, unventilated gyms. I've spent even more money than I care to reveal. It was December 2015, during a sweltering weekend of self-imposed purgatory, when I saw him.

At the time he was the best middle school basketball player I had ever seen! He bullied and finessed around the court at will. He was bigger, stronger, faster, and more skilled than any kid in the gym. He was built like a high school senior, but he hadn't even started high school. He was the kind of generational talent that would dominate at the next level and the next level after that. His name was Shemar Morrow.

The memory of Shemar is seared into my subconscious—that place that houses memories of shooting stars, rare anomalies, and other less-than-one-percent occurrences. Shemar's name is stored away in the same place as Stanley Johnson's—a name I would later hear as the eighth draft pick in the NBA draft. Like Stanley, I could imagine hearing Shemar's name announced as a draft pick. I did hear his name, but it wasn't during the NBA draft.

"Shemar Morrow is the most talented basketball player we have on this squad!" marveled Rob Robinson, the East Los Angeles Junior College assistant coach, as he watched Shemar in practice for the first time. Head Coach John Mosley and Coach Rob Robinson, featured on Netflix's docuseries *Last Chance U: Basketball Season 2*, were absolutely in love with Shemar's talent.

Last Chance U is exactly what it sounds like, a story that documents East Los Angeles Junior College's basketball recruits pursuing a last

CHAPTER 13

chance at their basketball dreams. The series chronicles players as they pursue their last chance to get a Division I basketball scholarship.

As we noted earlier, only about 1 percent of high school basketball players are fortunate enough to earn a Division I scholarship. The other 99 percent are left without an opportunity to advance their craft. That 99 percent also includes those who managed to earn a Division I scholarship but couldn't meet the academic, athletic, or behavioral rigor necessary to maintain that scholarship. For those individuals outside the 1 percent, options are limited. And one of those limited options is junior college.

Junior colleges are two-year schools that offer associate degrees and often have academic support that can be used as a bridge to a four-year institution. From a basketball perspective, junior colleges have an interesting mix of athletes. There are athletes who just weren't good enough for a Division I scholarship. There are high-level athletes who may have struggled academically. Some athletes played at programs that weren't a good fit. Although every East Los Angeles athlete arrives on campus under different circumstances, they all share one thing: this is their last chance to achieve their lifelong dream of playing Division I college basketball.

The National Collegiate Athletic Association, the collegiate version of ISU, groups American colleges and universities into different divisions based on overall competitiveness and resource allocation. Division I basketball offers the most athletic scholarship money and resources. However, there are other divisions too. Of the four-year institutions, college athletics is composed of Division I, Division II, Division III, and the National Association of Intercollegiate Athletics. But Division I is the level players dream about because it can be a potential launching pad to an NBA or WNBA career. And that's precisely what Shemar was hoping for: "When I was in, like, fifth grade, they was saying, like, I was the next LeBron. Like, I was to the league. Just all this stuff you hear.... I for sure thought I was fittin' to be, like, the number one pick in the draft by time 2021 came," he lamented in his opening introduction on *Last Chance U*. "I was for sure, for sure, like I was gon do one year of college, like, and I'm to the league for real. That's always been the plan, like I've always thought that's what I was going to do."

"I got to play at least one NBA game. I got to," Shemar added sadly, as if he were trying to convince himself that the possibility still existed. "I was going bad s—, or you just broke for real. I got to get back to hooping."

Time didn't diminish Shemar's talent. Even though he lamented the opportunity that seemed to pass him by, his game was just as electrifying as it was at the USA Basketball trial as a freshman. He recalls trying out for the under-sixteen USA Basketball national team and competing with the likes of Kevin Knox, Trae Young, and Jalen Green—all of whom subsequently made it to the NBA.

Shemar's talent even impressed the East Los Angeles Head Coach John Mosley, who said on *Last Chance U*, "He was one of the best players on the floor, so that got my attention. All right, I know he can help us. I know I want him here."

With so much positivity about his potential, why was Shemar in junior college? Why would a young phenom, who had the potential to be the next LeBron James, require a second chance? After all, his scouting evaluation was quite different from Stephen Curry's.

At twelve, Shemar was predicted to be a potential first-round draft pick. He was so good that anyone who saw him play immediately saw his professional potential; they didn't even talk about college. It was the same for Shemar; college was simply a stepping stone. He never talked about which academic subjects he was interested in or what he wanted as a potential major. Shemar's sole focus was professional basketball.

Why wasn't Shemar recruited to a Division I basketball program? He answered honestly on *Last Chance U*, and you could feel the pain in his tone: "I'm still trying to get my credits…. I don't know what it was…. Honestly, bro, it was grades, it was grades. My grades just wasn't good."

Shemar talked about grades as if they were something as fixed as a player's height—an independent variable beyond his control. He didn't believe that about basketball. For basketball, there was practice and hard work and getting better. But for grades? Shemar conceded that he had no control over them, even though he had control over them.

Speaking to Shermar, Mosley recounts in *Last Chance U*, "But look at where you at, you at East LA College. There's a reason why you here. There's some issues that we need to try to fix so that we can help you get to the next level."

Mosley took pride in his life's calling, which was helping these young men overcome their challenges. And that's what he was hoping to do with Shemar. Shemar's story was far from over. His journey as a basketball player wasn't so different from thousands of other young men and women who hope to achieve the American Dream. His journey as a young man is blessed by his version of Bob McKillop—Coach John Mosley.

The Shemar Morrow paradox, just like other paradoxes, isn't as uncommon as one would think. Looking back at our data, we see the convention that ensnared Shemar. Like other African American kids, he failed to see what the data showed. He was convinced that his success in the world depended on basketball. In Shermar's mind, his American Dream could only happen on the court. He didn't dream of becoming a doctor or engineer, even though the likelihood of becoming a doctor or engineer is sixty times more likely than becoming a professional basketball player.

Unfortunately, African Americans are underrepresented in both engineering and medicine. Even with that underrepresentation, those careers are still—by percentage—more accessible than playing in the NBA. The total number of African American engineers and physicians is higher than the total number of African American professional basketball players. But that fact is difficult for young student athletes and their parents to discern, and that discernment was embarrassingly difficult for Shemar.

Being a great basketball player requires practice and training. Being a great student requires that same dedication. Shemar, like thousands of other young athletes, was infatuated with the athlete component of the student athlete. There are no press conferences for medical school graduates, and they don't have special signing days for engineers. We live in a society where gladiators are celebrated, and scholars are tolerated. Shemar recognized that his grades were a disadvantage for his recruitment, but he failed to recognize that his grades could've been an advantage for just about everything else.

Twelve-year-old Shemar couldn't comprehend that success in life was more than just being a good basketball player. With everyone focusing on how great he was at basketball, he couldn't focus on how great he could have been at life. Even as he entered his adult years, his societal brainwashing remained ingrained. In his mind, his only options were doing something bad or getting back to hooping. His monocular focus was so myopic that he was still trying to complete his high school diploma—in junior college.

At some point, accountability for Shemar's outcomes rests with Shemar, but we shouldn't ignore the paradox that contributed to his way of thinking. When paradoxes hinder greatness, they're an inconvenience. When paradoxes hinder psychological and social development—especially in young and vulnerable populations—they can be disastrous.

Shemar's road was difficult, not because he wasn't good enough at basketball. Shemar's road was difficult because basketball allowed him to avoid the structure necessary to succeed as an adult. The travesty here isn't that society convinced him early on that basketball was his path to success. The travesty here is that society convinced him that basketball was his *only* path to success. Shemar said it himself: "I got to get back to hooping."

Coach Mosley was distraught by his inability to turn Shemar's story around, saying in one *Last Chance U* episode,

> He's been at a different home since, like, the sixth grade. I mean, he's staying with a family out in Orange County. It's an hour-and-a-half train ride. He squats on different couches.... There's so much instability, man. It's hard to even get to basketball. I can't even get to coaching him.

We can accomplish remarkable things as a society if we don't predetermine who can become a CEO or if we allow runners to use their specific advantage. We can accomplish so much more by creating an environment where kids such as Shemar understand the many ways it's possible to succeed. We should let the Shemar Morrows of tomorrow know there is a better chance of being a doctor or engineer than the next LeBron James. We should be sure to let the Shemar Morrows of tomorrow know there's ten times more money available for academic scholarships than athletic ones. We should let the Shemar Morrows of tomorrow know they could earn a potential $16 million in a lifetime without professional sports. If we focused on mitigating paradoxes like these, maybe Shemar would have had a better first chance and wouldn't need a last chance. As Assistant Coach Rob Robinson said in *Last Chance U*,

> Shemar did incredibly well at the beginning of our season because there was no structure. The moment there was structure, Shemar fell apart, and that's in his life as well.... Everyone who's told him to do something basketball-wise were telling him to do something for that moment in basketball. It was never to prepare Shemar for college or beyond. If he can go house to house, couch to couch, city to city, and play, he's fine. Structure? It's not going to work for him. But structure is the only thing that's going to help this fool for the next sixty years of his life.

CHAPTER 14

Disruptors

Disruptors don't have to discover something new; they just have to discover a practical use for new discoveries.

–Jay Samit

The New York Giants, Surya Bonaly, Roger Boisjoly, Stephen Curry, Usain Bolt, and Dr. Michael Berger are all disruptors. Whether they understood their role or not, they upended paradoxes and forced everyone to reconsider the conventions upon which their respective worlds were built. Each of these disruptors embodies an independently unique combination of characteristics that separates them from the status quo.

While they're all different, disruptors are unified in their unwillingness to accept things as they are. In that way, disruptors are disagreeable.

LESS THAN ONE PERCENT

Rules, conventions, and traditions make them bristle. Surya Bonaly spoke very openly about this during a radio interview for WBUR.[71]

> It happened too much. Also, because I was a woman. I think if I would have been a man and did the same thing, it would have been OK, because, "He's a guy, he's a dude." Because a woman was supposed to be dressed cute and shut up and just accept it. And, at this point, I'm like, "I don't care what kind of sex I belong to, I need to show that should not happen anymore."

She elaborated on this theme in a *Time* article in February 2022.[72]

> When you know how to do some elements, you always try to raise the bar and do something different, and not stick to the same things forever. I thought it would be good for me, because I was also very athletic, I could just try and work on quad jumps."

But why? Why would Surya be compelled to "always try to raise the bar and do something different"? If high-level athletes are always looking for a competitive edge, why didn't all of Surya's competitive counterparts push those same limits and raise their respective bars?

The difference between Surya and her peers rests in the difference between their goals. Most of her competitors were striving to be the best skater they could be. Surya, on the other hand, was obsessed with being *better* than the best skater she could be. That small difference is monumental!

---

71 "'Please, Try to Be Fair': Surya Bonaly Confronts 1994 World Championships Loss," WBUR, March 7, 2019, https://www.wbur.org/onpoint/2019/03/07/surya-bonaly-skating-losers-netflix.

72 Park, "Quadruple Jumps Are Transforming Women's Figure Skating."

CHAPTER 14

Surya likely found it mind-numbingly mundane to incrementally increase the proficiency of her standard elements. Instead, she raised the bar by inventing creatively disruptive *new* elements. She raised the bar by being the first woman to attempt a quad—a jump that features four full rotations before a skater lands. And she raised the bar by attempting and landing an "illegal" backflip in front of an incensed establishment. That disagreeableness comes from a disdain for the status quo, a contempt for tradition, and an uncomfortableness with the comfort of painting within the lines.

Disagreeableness isn't something that disruptors do to gain an advantage. Disagreeableness is fundamental to who they are. Even when those actions cause grave consequences—such as doing a backflip in competition and dropping to tenth place—being disagreeable provides freedom from their real or perceived constraints.

"That's cool. I can do it, and nobody is gonna yell at me. I will be just free. Do what I want. It's cool!" Bonaly said in her thick French accent, giddy as she answered the question from the Champions on Ice commentator in the Netflix documentary *Losers*. She was free! She was a disruptor who was no longer confined to painting inside the lines. That lack of constraint gave her more satisfaction than winning ever could.

Her refusal to take the podium and wear the silver medal wasn't just a manifestation of her second-place anger. Her refusal was a reaction to receiving second place *after* she pushed the envelope. Disagreeableness isn't only an impulsive disdain for convention. It's also a compulsion driven by a need for change. Surya was sad, but she also was angry. She was angry at the lack of appreciation for her struggle. And after learning more about her, you'll understand why.

After her birth in Nice in 1973, Surya was placed in an orphanage. She was adopted at eight months and spent most of her early years on a farm without running water or electricity. Her adoptive parents prided themselves on being 100 percent self-sustaining and self-sufficient. When she wasn't contributing to the family farm chores—which wasn't very often—she had an extensive extracurricular regimen. She practiced the flute, fencing, ballet, horseback riding, and diving. Her mom created structure and regimen for her expansive interests, and she was also Surya's skating coach.

Surya's unique upbringing had another intriguing element. Surya, whose birth mother was from Réunion and whose birth father was from Côte d'Ivoire, was Black. Her adoptive parents were White. Although it was illegal at the time for the French state to collect ethnic demographic data, saying that France in the 1970s lacked diversity is a gross understatement. When Surya started skating in 1975, being a Black skater was as far away from the skating standard as one could get.

Surya's story gives us a little insight into her disagreeableness. As an adopted Black child in a predominantly White country, in a predominantly White sport, living on a self-sufficient isolated farm, she might see the world differently than the ISU. In her Andscape interview, Surya said, "Outside of how well the skater jumps or spins, what are you judging them on? How well you like their legs, their dresses? It's too difficult."[73] When Surya refused to stand on the second-place podium she believed didn't belong to her, one can only imagine her difficulty coping with that Barry O'Shea moment.

Surya didn't create something new. She simply found an application for something she'd already seen. Surya didn't invent the backflip, nor did she invent the quadruple jump. Male skaters had been attempting and landing quads long before she attempted hers. Surya wasn't the first to land a backflip either. She was, however, the first woman to attempt a quadruple jump in competition and the first to land a backflip on one foot.

---

73 Mathewson, "Former Olympian Surya Bonaly Says Don't Call Her a Rebel."

CHAPTER 14

If Surya had focused on perfecting the artistry of figure skating instead of raising the bar and trying something different, she would likely have fared better. But that's not how disruptors are wired. For disruptors, winning is important, but only when winning is an outcome of disruption. Surya's reaction to narrowly losing two consecutive world championships was to continue to push the envelope—which meant doing more of the things that caused her to narrowly lose two consecutive world championships. She doubled down on disruption, even though that disruption is precisely what the judges didn't want.

While disruptors may not always get the result they want, their disruption can change the trajectory of their sport, genre, or business. Thanks to Surya's disruption, the number of men and women attempting quadruple jumps exploded. And her banned illegal backflip is now commonly seen on the professional circuit and is ironically called "the Bonaly." Just as Stephen Curry altered the world of basketball, and Usain Bolt forced track off its track, Surya changed skating forever.

Sports aren't the only disciplines susceptible to disruption. Paradoxes exist in every field, genre, and niche. Each year CNBC creates a list of the top fifty disruptive companies in the world. This list is a who's who of next-generation companies poised to dominate their respective industries. In an article written on May 17, 2022, CNBC reported, "All told, these firms have raised a half-trillion dollars in venture capital. At least 41 are unicorns, with valuations of $1 billion or more—14 are valued at over $10 billion."[74]

CNBC compiles its list using a proprietary process that quantifies a company's disruptive potential. Specifically, companies are

---

[74] "The 2022 CNBC Disruptor 50 List: Meet the Next Generation of Silicon Valley," CNBC, updated May 1, 2023, https://www.cnbc.com/2022/05/17/these-are-the-2022-cnbc-disruptor-50-companies.html.

ranked "by importance and ability to disrupt established industries and public companies."[75]

CNBC is looking for the business version of Surya Bonaly. In their search for business disruptors, CNBC is looking for companies attempting quad jumps and landing backflips on one leg. CNBC is looking for those companies because they know that companies that push the envelope will change entire industries. Let's look at CNBC's 2022 list of the top fifty most disruptive companies.[76]

Rank	Company	Description
1	Flexport	Overwhelming the supply chain bottleneck
2	Brex	The start-up world's finance department
3	Lineage Logistics	On top of the global food supply's temperature
4	Canva	The feature presentation
5	Guild Education	Work. Study.
6	Convoy	Trucking as we've known it stops here
7	Blockchain.com	Web3's dot com
8	Stripe	Making the internet pay
9	Dapper Labs	The shot Michael Jordan and Kevin Durant are taking on decentralization.
10	Pony.ai	Hand over the reins.
11	Checkout.com	A rival to the Stripe swipe
12	Chime	Challenger bank in the fintech market
13	Discord	How digital natives converse
14	Flock Freight	Fully loaded
15	Medable	The virtual clinical trials
16	Truepill	The infrastructure for online pharmacy
17	Arctic Wolf	A cyber defender from up north
18	CloudTrucks	Big ideas for the Big Road
19	Maven Clinic	Putting women first in health
20	Monarch Tractor	1 driver. 8 tractors. All electric.
21	Fanatics	Taking sports merch into the metaverse
22	Tala	The world's local lender
23	Anduril Industries	Engineering an autonomous military arsenal
24	Workato	Office work automated
25	Lacework	Cybercrime's lie detector

75 CNBC, "The 2022 CNBC Disrupter 50 List."

76 CNBC, "The 2022 CNBC Disrupter 50 List."

CHAPTER 14

Rank	Company	Description
26	Somatus	Kidney care without the dialysis centers
27	Gopuff	All your instant needs fulfilled
28	Virta Health	Don't treat diabetes; reverse it.
29	Zipline	A life-saving drone, with a Walmart side hustle
30	CarbonCure	Carbon to concrete
31	Jüsto	Mexico's answer to Walmart
32	Biobot Analytics	A wastewater virus hunter
33	Airtable	The code for every knowledge worker
34	Databricks	The start-up world's biggest data bet
35	DataRobot	A one-trillion predictions market maker
36	Relativity Space	An Elon Musk reusable rocket competitor
37	NEXT Insurance	Digital small business insurance
38	Ro	Planning to be a digital health survivor
39	Airspace	Critical on-demand delivery for the pandemic era
40	Thrasio	Consumer products giant for the digital age
41	Cybereason	A bird's eye view
42	BlocPower	Building net-zero cities
43	OURA	The one ring to rule wearables
44	MoonPay	The biggest celebrity bet on crypto
45	Zum	School bus magic
46	Exotec	France's warehouse robot unicorn
47	Plaid	A bridge from fintech to bank
48	Cityblock Health	Health tech for low-income America
49	Impossible Foods	From plant-based fad to fixture
50	Envoy	Back to the office of the future

Like Silicon Valley start-ups, business disruptors spend most of their creative time searching for the business equivalent of a convention. Investors give millions of dollars to innovative start-ups because of their ability to build a company around disrupting a specific convention. That's the formula for a successful start-up.

Typically, established companies share their revenue and profitability as a measure of success. Because early-stage companies are so new, revenue isn't always an accurate measure of a new company's potential. Considering that fact, how do the journalists at CNBC and potential investors evaluate a start-up's future worth?

The most disruptive companies, and therefore the ones with the highest likelihood of succeeding in the future, find a convention and turn it inside out. For example, Zum challenges the school bus industry convention by using cloud computing and machine learning to increase efficiency and decrease cost. Like Dr. Berger, Cityblock believed that the healthcare convention was failing patients. Specifically, Cityblock focused on low-income and elderly patients with limited access to healthcare. Zipline uses autonomous vehicles, robots, and drones to disrupt medical supply logistics and bring lifesaving medical supplies to remote regions. During the COVID-19 pandemic, they helped Ghana deliver one million vaccine doses.[77]

Lastly, Guild Education is transforming educational student debt. Traditionally, money is required to get an education, an education is required to get a job, and a job is required to make money. Education financing is illogically circular. Guild Education is disrupting that standard by moving education into the work environment. Instead of getting an education to be able to get a job, the founders at Guild Education believe in getting a job to be able to get an education.

These are just a few examples of companies and the conventions they disrupt. Disruptors, whether they're individuals or companies, behave similarly. Like Surya, their role in their respective industries is to raise the bar. But just like skating, the business world has its own stoic judging panel. There are two sets of judges in business: consumers and investors. Because it's difficult for smaller, newer companies to

---

[77] "Zipline Delivers 1 Million COVID-19 Vaccines in Ghana," sUAS News, accessed June 26, 2024, https://www.suasnews.com/2022/03/zipline-delivers-1-million-covid-19-vaccines-in-ghana/.

CHAPTER 14

have a large consumer base, they rely heavily on investors. The good news for them is this: investors love disruptors.

According to CNBC,[78] Zipline raised $486 million and at the time had a valuation of $2.5 billion. Guild Education raised $378.5 million and was valued at $3.7 billion. Zum raised $208 million and was valued at $937 million. Cityblock Health raised $868.8 million and was valued at $6.3 billion. These investors were very different from their judging counterparts in Nagano. Fortunately, business disruptions are better received than figure skating disruptions, and they have a track record to prove it. The year 2022 wasn't the first time CNBC created a list of the top fifty disruptors. Let's look back at CNBC's 2018 list of fifty disruptors.[79]

---

78 CNBC, "The 2022 CNBC Disrupter 50 List."

79 "A Look Back at the CNBC Disruptor 50: 6 Years, 167 Companies," CNBC, updated January 29, 2020, https://www.cnbc.com/2018/05/22/a-look-back-at-the-cnbc-disruptor-50-6-years-167-companies.html.

LESS THAN ONE PERCENT

Rank	Company	Description
1	SpaceX	Taking the lead in the new space race.
2	Uber	Faring better in the post-Travis era.
3	Airbnb	Rewriting the book on bookings.
4	Didi Chuxing	How do you say "Uber" in Mandarin?
5	Lyft	Sticking to the high road.
6	Grab	Just another rideshare unicorn...
7	23andMe	A genetics house call.
8	Udacity	Nanodegree your way to a new job.
9	Rent the Runway	A closet in the cloud.
10	Coinbase	The future of money is here.
11	TransferWise	Eating up foreign-exchange fees.
12	Oscar Health	Health insurance that actually works for you.
13	Payoneer	Helping companies get paid around the world.
14	SurveyMonkey	A way to better answers.
15	Progyny	Fertile ground for disruption.
16	Adyen	The company that gave PayPal the wooden shoe.
17	TheRealReal	What's in your closet?
18	Indigo Agriculture	Seeding the world.
19	Exetap	Powering India's cashless revolution.
20	Peloton	A new spin on spinning.
21	Ginkgo Bioworks	Microbe economics.
22	LISNR	No Wi-Fi? No problem.
23	WeWork	For when you need some space.
24	Ellevest	Wall Street for women.
25	Zipline International	Drones to the rescue.

CHAPTER 14

Rank	Company	Description
26	LanzaTech	Won't let carbon go to waste.
27	Crowdstrike	Into the breach.
28	Xiaomi	A $100 billion iPhone competitor.
29	Flirtey	The robot revolution takes flight.
30	Veritas Genetics	Your whole genome.
31	Houzz	Improving home improvement.
32	C3 IoT	What are those devices saying?
33	Palantir Technologies	They know you.
34	Darktrace	A digital immune boost.
35	Duolingo	How do you say...
36	Pinterest	100 billion ideas shared.
37	Thinx	An underwear innovator takes on Tampax.
38	Robinhood	Turning trading upside down.
39	Uptake	Big machines break.
40	Drawbridge	An ad's journey from screen to screen.
41	InMobi	A personalized mobile ad experience.
42	Coursera	We don't need no formal IT education.
43	Stripe	Cracking the code on getting your interest business paid.
44	Illumio	We all have vulnerabilities.
45	Fanatics	They root for everyone.
46	Auris Health	A surgical robot pioneer scrubs in.
47	Luminar	How self-driving cars see around corners.
48	Apeel Sciences	The end of rotten food.
49	GitHub	The ultimate source for open source.
50	SoFi	Bank, borrow, and invest—all in one app.

Business disruption is vastly different from figure skating disruption. (Bear with me a moment—we're going to come back to this list.) Do you remember the reaction to Surya's ultimate disruption? The crowd was amazed, and the commentators were thrilled. And the judges? They were incensed!

In the figure skating paradox, the people responsible for evaluating performance were also responsible for maintaining the convention. Surya wasn't being evaluated for the beauty of her artistry. She was being evaluated for how her picture, beautiful or not, stayed within the lines. Business, however, has an entirely different construct.

The business world reacts differently to disruptors because those who judge the performance aren't the ones maintaining the convention. The competitive market judges companies based on their ability to disrupt. If Surya were a business disruptor, she would have been judged by the crowd, not the judges. She would have never been penalized for performing a backflip. Frankly, if Surya were a start-up, she would have raised millions.

A Bonaly backflip-based start-up is theoretical, but the list of CNBC companies is very real. While the 2022 list of top fifty disruptors is filled with companies known to private equity fund managers, the 2018 list is much more intriguing. Here are a few sentences to illustrate how these companies fared.

After watching the *SpaceX* launch, we took an *Uber* or *Lyft* to our *Airbnb*. The next morning, after my *Peloton*, I received a *SurveyMonkey* about my experience. Then I went to work at *WeWork*, where I exchanged cryptocurrency through *Coinbase* and traded stocks with *Robinhood*. And to relax, I spend time on *Pinterest* before opening up my *23andMe* results. I hope my Michael Jordan jersey from *Fanatics* is arriving soon.

These companies went from a formulaic list of disruptors to a list of familiar household names. In a relatively short time, these companies have gone from disagreeable upstarts to names we use in lieu of the conventions they disrupted. Uber and Lyft disagreed with and disrupted the taxicab convention. Airbnb disagreed with and disrupted the hotel convention. WeWork disagreed with and disrupted the office convention. Robinhood disagreed with and disrupted the stock purchase convention and so on. Investors invested millions in disagreeable disruptive companies that became companies that make billions.

As a trait, disagreeableness is a quality that many find undesirable. After all, wouldn't agreeableness be better? To understand why something as undesirable as disagreeableness would be a positive thing for disruptors, we should consider what it means to agree. According to *Merriam-Webster*, agreeing means to accept, concede, or concur. To be agreeable is tantamount to groupthink, where everyone agrees with the prevailing convention or consensus. Conversely, disagreeability leads to disruption, and disruption leads to progress.

Disruption isn't only for tech-savvy Ivy League dropouts. Raising the bar starts with identifying conventions and developing ways to disrupt them. Incremental improvement isn't disruption. There are wildly successful blue-chip companies that focus primarily on improving efficiencies or creating a better product. Those are good business practices, but they aren't disruptive.

Justin Gatlin, the last American to win the gold in the Olympic one-hundred-meter dash in 2004, was one of the best at mastering track conventions. He was successful—until the emergence of disruptor Usain Bolt. When it comes to greatness, doing things better isn't always better than doing things differently.

Start-ups are created by identifying areas that need disruption. Successful start-ups are creating products and services that execute that disruptive hypothesis. The stickiness of the company—how long it lasts and how well it does in the market—is directly proportional to the degree of disruption. Uber, for example, has decimated the traditional taxi business by revolutionizing the business of moving people. From the taxi driver's perspective, that disruption was devastating. From the people-movement perspective, Uber has changed the world.

Disruption moves markets, revolutionizes genres, and even creates new categories. Disruptors are so vital that CNBC highlights fifty of the best every year. But if disruptors are so important to the world's progress, why aren't they more eagerly embraced? Why are there so many paradoxes and conventions if disruptions are indeed positive? Why did the judges react the way they did to Surya's disruption?

Disruptors live in a weird entanglement of paradox. Although so many positives result from breaking conventions, being a disruptor is isolating. The 2018 list of top disruptors includes many companies that have challenged the market and thrived in their new disruptive spaces. However, it also lists many companies that didn't survive the market's reaction to their backflips.

More disruptive start-ups fail than succeed. Indeed, disruption is fraught with risk and a high likelihood of failure. For skaters, sprinters, and NBA teams, it's far safer to try to get better faster than the others are trying to get better, to avoid getting worse. Improving one's performance relative to a standard, convention, or consensus is far more likely to result in a competitive outcome. That's why disruption is so lonely. That's why Surya was so emotionally distraught and refused to follow another convention and stand on the podium.

If you want to compete, then doing what NBA teams are doing makes sense. Every team in the league uses the same tactic to gain an advantage over every other team. This creates what sports pundits call competitive equity. For the NBA, competitive equity increases revenue because fans everywhere believe they have a chance to win each year. If your team has a chance to win, fans watch more games, and teams generate more television revenue. Close adherence to skating conventions increases the likelihood of *edging* out your competition—not because you're the best skater but because you're the best skater relative to the ISU standard.

CHAPTER 14

Disruptors aren't trying to compete. They aren't trying to incrementally improve their way to the convention. Disruptors are chasing greatness, and that's a vastly different pursuit. Stabilizers—those who pride themselves on competing within a convention—try to paint the best picture they can within the lines.

In the corporate world, stabilizers are the chief operating and financial officers. They're responsible for managing the minutiae necessary to sustain that competitive approach. For stabilizers, failure means you weren't good enough, or you didn't adhere to the standards well enough. Their grind is focused on the quality of the product and the efficiency of the process. Stabilizers are essential to the world. They're an intricate part of almost every organization. Stabilizers are often successful within conventions. Just ask Yuka Sato.

If we look at Sato's upbringing, we can postulate why she became such a successful stabilizer. Her parents, Nobuo Sato and Kumiko Okawa, were both Olympic figure skaters who competed in the 1960s. Both of Sato's parents trained the young Japanese phenom in the art of figure skating. As competitors themselves, they taught Yuka to paint beautiful pictures within the lines. This upbringing starkly contrasts with that of a young African girl, given up by her birth mother and adopted by a French family who lived on a farm off the grid and who competed in a sport where she was the only Black participant.

But not every stabilizer is as successful as Yuka Sato. Many stabilizers struggle with the constant incremental improvement required to compete. Just ask Shemar Morrow. His paradox put him in an almost impossible situation. He was thrust into a stabilizer role at an early age by everyone's consensus. Unfortunately, as far as stabilizers go, he wasn't a particularly good one. Shemar had all the talent in the world, but his Achilles' heel—structure—made him struggle as a stabilizer.

129

Remember, Shemar excelled at the beginning of the season when there was no structure. That would have worked if he was a disruptor. Unfortunately, as a stabilizer, he was ill-equipped for the task of trying to get better faster than the other players were getting better. When Shemar had that competitive structure, he fell apart.

Structure challenged Shemar so much that he even struggled to get his high school diploma. Conventions and their ability to inappropriately delineate winners and losers boxed Shemar into a space where he couldn't compete. Shemar was horrible at painting within the lines. Because he didn't get better faster than the other players were getting better, he fell further and further behind.

From *CNBC's* data, we can see that being a business disruptor is still challenging—even in an environment that rewards disruption. On June 20, 2018, *Forbes* magazine published a survey of four hundred executives focused on disruptors and their returns. In this survey they identified that about 37 percent of companies considered themselves disruptors. This data was compiled by the Forbes Insights and Treasure Data survey, which "includes the views and experiences of 400 executives across key industry segments."[80]

Interestingly, 51 percent of executives felt their organizations were at risk because of industry disruption by start-ups. Though many executives believed their companies were at greater risk because disruptors were entering their space, very few were willing to become disruptors themselves. Even in business, where disruption is accepted and rewarded, they avoided disruption and settled for trying not to fall behind.

---

80 "New Forbes Insights Report Shows Organizations Feel Customer Data Is Siloed and Exclusionary," *Forbes*, June 20, 2018, https://www.forbes.com/sites/forbespr/2018/06/20/new-forbes-insights-report-shows-organizations-feel-customer-data-is-siloed-and-exclusionary/?sh=4c4371da299b.

CHAPTER 14

It's clear that success is possible by meticulously painting within the lines. It's also clear that meticulously painting within the lines is unlikely to produce greatness. Stabilizers and disruptors are both competing to win, but the way they compete is profoundly different. Stabilizers compete with others, while disruptors compete with themselves. Disruptors want to win but only when winning allows the pursuit of greatness. And when winning and greatness collide, they do illegal backflips.

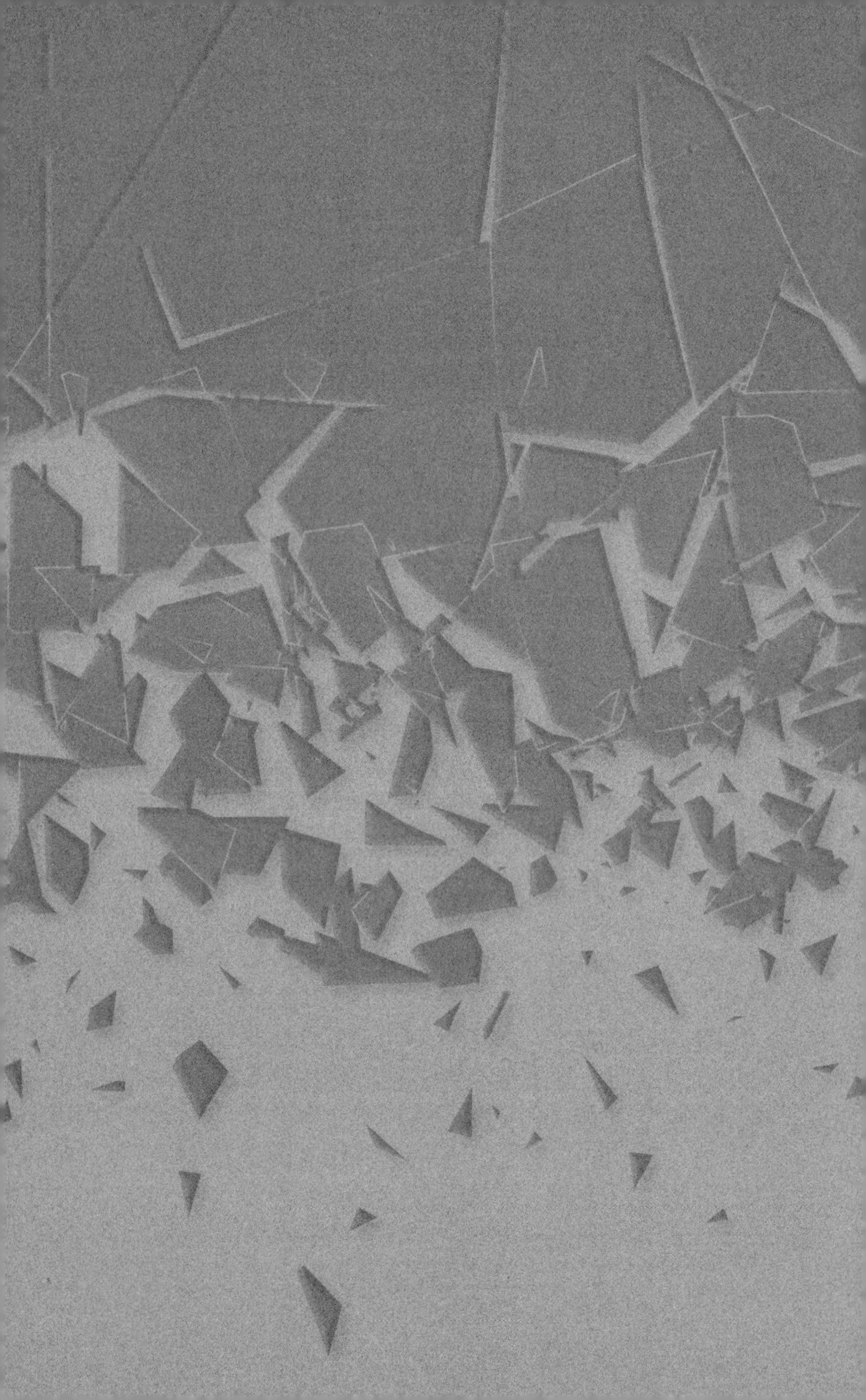

CHAPTER 15

Scary Giraffe

You have to live through the worst parts of your life, so you never take the best parts for granted.

–Unknown

Having children is one of life's most fulfilling events. But it is also one of life's most challenging undertakings. In some ways children are genetically randomized facsimiles of their parents. In other ways they're nothing like their parents and try their best not to be.

The goal of any parent is to ensure their child's future, and that task requires sacrifice. I was definitely in that camp. I would sacrifice anything for my kids. I would sacrifice everything for my kids. And early in my parenting journey, I would learn exactly what sacrifice meant.

I remember it like it was yesterday. I got a call at work. My four-year-old son was in an ambulance on his way to the emergency room.

LESS THAN ONE PERCENT

It wasn't clear what happened. His grandmother, who was with him at the time, described the episode. She was in the other room and heard him yell, and then she found him on his back. His eyes were rolled back into his head, and his arms and legs were twitching. He looked like he was holding his breath and wouldn't respond to his name. He was having a seizure.

About 470,000 kids in America have active epilepsy.[81] Epilepsy is a neurologic disorder where the electrical activity of the brain—which, under normal conditions, is coordinated and structured—becomes erratic and chaotic. That brain misfiring results in what medical science calls a seizure. Seizures can have multiple forms, from staring spells to shaking of an isolated limb. But the kind of seizure that most people associate with epilepsy is a grand mal seizure. Also known as a generalized tonic-clonic seizure, a grand mal seizure causes loss of consciousness and violent uncoordinated muscle contractions, followed by a period of prolonged unresponsiveness. This sequence of events would be challenging for any person to endure—and it would be even more challenging for a four-year-old little boy.

There's something absolutely unsettling about your child being sick. Every second that ticks by feels like an hour. It's no wonder that Dr. Berger wanted to decrease the time that patients waited for emergency care. Fortunately, all the tests came back without revealing any significant underlying illness. We took him home, comforted by the fact that this was a one-time anomaly. As worried as we were, we were just as relieved to be home.

And then it happened.

---

81 Matthew M. Zack and Rosemarie Kobau, "National and State Estimates of the Numbers of Adults and Children with Active Epilepsy—United States, 2015," Centers for Disease Control and Prevention, August 11, 2017, https://www.cdc.gov/mmwr/volumes/66/wr/mm6631a1.htm.

CHAPTER 15

Several weeks after that first episode, he had another seizure—and then another and another and another. There were days when he seized so much that he couldn't eat. Imagine following your four-year-old around the house all day, worried he'll fall unconscious with his arms and legs shaking violently. He woke up crying, and we cried with him. Before realizing where he was and what was going on, he seized again.

All told, he would have over five hundred seizures in less than nine months. He was in the hospital more than he was in school. He lost weight because he wasn't awake long enough to eat. Each seizure was followed by a period of somnolence, called a postictal phase. Between the seizures and his postictal phase, he spent entire days unconscious.

My son had it the worst, but everyone in the family was shaken, none more shaken than his two-year-old little sister. Most families spend their time going to school, eating dinner together, and watching cartoon movies. Our family time was preoccupied with admissions to the hospital, magnetic resonance scans, encephalograms, and neurology appointments.

As hard as it was to deal with as adults, the impact on his sister was even worse. She went from playing with her brother, riding bikes, and convincing him to steal cookies to watching everybody in the family crying and running to his aid. She saw his seizures, and I'm still unsure how those events got processed through the mind of a two-year-old.

It was clear she was aware that her brother, whom she called "Bubby," was really sick. We noticed that during this time, she would carry a stuffed giraffe. She took it everywhere. This was odd because she wasn't the kind of kid who carried around stuffed animals. In retrospect, I don't think we fully appreciated the psychological impact on a two-year-old who looked up to her larger-than-life big brother.

She didn't cry or complain. She would rub his head while he slept. Fortunately, he rarely seized in his sleep. She was as supportive as you could ever imagine a two-year-old could be, considering she couldn't comprehend the gravity of the moment. That giraffe embodied the immature emotion of a two-year-old worried about her "Bubby." When she couldn't find it, she would walk around the house saying, "Scary Giraffe."

My son's seizure disorder was a different kind of disruption. It changed everyone in the family—our lifestyle, work schedules, and relationships all changed. We all learned to paint outside the lines. To this day I don't believe that we've all fully recovered. At the time I didn't fully appreciate that my perspective on parenting was flawed. Like most parents, I had aspirations for my children. But those aspirations weren't *their* aspirations. Without knowing it, I expected my children to paint between my lines. I had created a convention that a seizure disorder was more than happy to disrupt. I wanted the best for them but didn't realize that parenting is about helping them find what's best for them.

All my plans, dreams, and hopes for my son went out the window. I had to learn to accept him for who he was. And at that time, he was a child with a debilitating seizure disorder. Whatever overrated Ivy League plan I had in my mind got replaced by prayers for him to have regular days. For our family, regular days—days without seizures—were exceptional. Instead of career, sport, or academic expectations, I longed for those seizure-free moments.

Surya, Steph, and Bolt disrupted long-standing conventions. However, disruptors aren't always individuals searching for greatness. Like my son's seizure disorder, disruptors can present as isolated events or a series of occurrences over time. The dot-com boom of the nineties was a disruptor. It's theorized that an asteroid hit the earth, and the resultant explosion caused the extinction of the dinosaurs.

The dinosaurs were fatally disrupted, not by an individual but by an event. Disruptive events are similar to individual disruptors. Their presence disrupts conventions and forces those they disrupt to think and operate differently. Those events create environments that challenge the status quo. And those dependent on the status quo for survival risk extinction if they fail to adapt.

Our ability to change and grow depends on our ability to handle disruption and shed our preconceived conventions. Like the CEOs from the *Forbes* article, most people know what disruption looks like but struggle to embody its characteristics. After disruption, stabilizers try to find ways to get back to normal. Disruptors, on the other hand, use disruption to propel themselves to a new and drastically different normal.

The characteristic most necessary for managing through a disruptive event isn't toughness, resilience, or strength. The essential characteristic of enduring a disruptive event is humility. The *Cambridge Dictionary* defines humility "as the feeling or attitude that you have no special importance that makes you better than others." That humility is necessary to release one's stranglehold on conventions.

Why were Surya's judges so incensed? They were incensed because they felt they had special importance. Being a judge in a world championship skating contest—so important they call it the Worlds—is far from a job that has no special importance. When challenged by a disruptor painting outside the lines, they had no choice but to react the way they did. They lacked the humility necessary to recognize that they had just witnessed greatness.

Humility allows moments of self-introspection, which allows an analysis of the conventions we inappropriately hold dear. My son's horrible seizure disruption forced me to examine my parenting conventions. I realized that much of what I wanted for him was my interpretation of his life based on my conventions. Those moments of humility changed my life. They changed my work conventions and my relationship conventions.

The adage "what doesn't kill you makes you stronger" is partially incorrect. Regarding disruptions, that adage is more correctly stated, what doesn't kill you makes you humble. What doesn't kill you makes you different. What doesn't kill you makes you examine every convention you took for granted.

My son doesn't fully remember that horrible time. I appreciate the successful journey he's on now. The best part about his journey is that it's *his* journey. And my daughter? She has no recollection of her Bubby's seizures. What about Scary Giraffe? What about the inanimate friend that enabled a two-year-old to get through one of the worst disruptions in her young life? She can't remember it at all. And I can't forget.

CHAPTER 16

NANNY

In order for the oppressed to be able to wage the struggle for their liberation, they must perceive the reality of oppression not as a closed world from which there is no exit, but as a limiting situation which they can transform. This perception is a necessary but not a sufficient condition for liberation; it must become the motivating force for liberating action.

–Paulo Freire

Disruptions don't just change the course of paradoxes. They can change the trajectory of lives, companies, and entire industries. The NBA's analytic paradox coincided with the Steph Curry evaluation paradox, which created an environment that forged the greatest three-point disruption of all time. Stephen Curry would have never become Steph Curry if the analytic revolution hadn't exponentially increased the NBA's reliance on his favorite shot. Paradoxes and their associated disruptions are predominantly dependent on timing.

When a paradox occurs is almost as important as the paradox itself. Different individuals with different strengths and weaknesses react to different situations in different ways. The consensus that Shemar Morrow was the best twelve-year-old basketball player in the country stifled his development. The opposite was true for Stephen Curry. The consensus that he *wasn't* considered the country's best high school basketball player propelled him to greatness.

Timing isn't the only factor that can alter a reaction to disruption. Doubt is another factor that does interesting things. For some, internal doubt forces introspection and can paradoxically motivate that individual. For others, internal doubt is destructive, leading to indecisiveness and a lack of confidence.

One who doubts oneself may work harder, longer, and more intensely to mitigate that doubt. In *Maniacal Fanaticism*, I describe the inward chip. In its simplest terms, the inward chip is self-doubt transformed into powerful and introspective motivation.

My professional coach's external doubt was a powerful motivator. It made me more confident and focused and increased my intensity. I wanted to prove him wrong. Ironically, his doubt about me as a future CEO improved my candidacy. That perceived slight is also represented in Jamaica's refrain, "Wi likkle but wi tallawah." This colloquialism has rallied an entire nation by embodying an underdog mentality.

Malcolm Gladwell's book *David and Goliath* is all about underdogs. He discusses how we misinterpret them—and how their disadvantages can often be advantages. Becoming a CEO, beating the greatest quarterback of all time *twice*, and landing a backflip on one foot are all examples of underdog overachievement.

The complex combination of a convention-laden paradox and a slight-driven disruptor is so potent. This combination requires the disagreeableness necessary to paint outside of the lines. Jamaica's track-and-field performance isn't that of a stabilizer getting better at a faster rate than everybody else. Its track-and-field performance is one of slight-driven disruption. Jamaica is focused on track-and-field greatness, not track-and-field competition.

Jamaica's disruptive mentality isn't only represented in its athletic pursuits. It's also evident in its music. Even if you aren't a music aficionado, you've likely heard of Jamaica's national music. A combination of early ska and rock steady, reggae's sound and singular uniqueness emerged in the early 1960s.

As a music genre, reggae is the only popular music to arise from such a small country. Postclassical music genres have almost exclusively originated in the United States. Rock and roll, hip-hop, rhythm and blues, and jazz can all be attributed to American musical ingenuity.

These music genres were generated at some of the most disruptive times in musical history. Broad rebellion in the United States against long-standing social conventions manifested itself in disruptive new music genres. Like most disruptions, many of these genres were initially shunned and criticized by the musical version of Surya's judges.

Throughout American history, musical disruption has directly correlated with society's decreasing tolerance for conventions. Women's rights, the Civil Rights Movement, the sexual revolution, and antiwar and antigovernment sentiment all fueled offbeat rhythms that rejected long-standing musical conventions.

Jazz took classical music and disrupted its structure—using previously off-putting chords as the jazz standard. Rap and hip-hop disrupted slow melodic singing and replaced it with poetic and rhythmic speeches over electronic beats. Rock and roll took calm, ordered reprises, and replaced them with loud drums, squealing guitars, and sexual innuendo. Music reflects the society it comes from. Hence, rock and roll, jazz, and rap emerged from the social disruption of America's fifties, sixties, and seventies.

Where does reggae fit in? In the shadow of America's disruptive dominance, how did a country of under three million people create a musical disruption of its own? Reggae's official launch was sometime in the late 1960s. Reggae's most popular band, Bob Marley's Wailers, hit the scene in 1963. The 1970s were a challenging period for Jamaica. Internally, the country was in political turmoil. The tension was heightened by gang affiliation and police corruption. Meanwhile, big brother America was navigating its own internal civil rights challenges.

That sociopolitical disruption connected Jamaica with the United States through reggae's biggest star—Robert Nesta Marley. Bob Marley, as most of the world knows him, was the most recognized icon of the reggae movement. Reggae was energetic and vibrant. The beat itself was so moving it was difficult to sit still while listening to it.

Before reggae, most popular music emphasized the first and third beats of each measure. Reggae, however, placed the emphasis on the second and fourth beats. This "upbeat" made reggae instantly recognizable. It was so musically unique that it was almost immediately placed in its own genre.

Bob and the Wailers used this technique, emphasizing the upbeats by adding guitar chords. What made Bob Marley's music even more unique was his songwriting. His unique voice belted out stories of oppression and social injustice. He didn't only tell stories about Jamaica. He also assaulted all things unfair and unjust worldwide. Using his platform, Marley encouraged the world to disrupt all oppressive societal conventions.

Marley's lyrics were melodic and rhythmic. They were filled with the pain of oppression and the power of a superstar. "Emancipate yourselves from mental slavery. None but ourselves can free our minds," he sang in "Redemption Song." This track was released in 1980, long after the height of the Civil Rights Movement. Why would Marley use those words? What mental slavery was he referring to?

Marley is referring to conventions and asking his listeners to emancipate themselves from their grasp. He's asking them to be disruptors. In this verse, "None but ourselves can free our mind," he's telling us that we have the responsibility to see paradoxes and disrupt the conventions that create them. One of the world's most popular artists—who financially benefitted from a world full of conventions—was asking the world to disrupt those same conventions. He was asking the world to help him in his search for truth.

Marley gives insight into his search for truth in an interview with Lionel "Bingie" Barker during the 1979 Survival Tour in Ottawa, Canada.[82]

> There's a force fighting against, not just the music but the truth. Yeah, because sometime the truth is like a two-edged sword. You know, it cut sharp. That mean plenty people don't like hear the truth. Because plenty people find themselves feeling guilty. So the truth is an offense.

---

82 reggaeman91, "Bob Marley Interview Lionel Bingie Barker 1979," January 27, 2010, YouTube, https://www.youtube.com/watch?v=6Svn48Uq9r4.

Bob was referring to the truth that is hidden by paradoxes. Paradoxes hide information behind fallacies and conventions. The truth is offensive because it causes people to feel guilty—that's the definition of groupthink. People feel guilty about being disagreeable. It's much easier to agree than to employ the necessary effort to dispel the paradox.

Jamaica's national Barry O'Shea manifests itself in a mantra that highlights how small Jamaica is and how big of an impact it has on the world. That perceived slight galvanized an entire nation around a national sport that—by sheer population—it should never excel in. That perceived slight also compelled Marley to search for truth. By his account, he was living in a world where truth was avoided because it cuts too sharp.

Marley isn't only a musical icon. Both Jamaicans and non-Jamaicans alike adorn him with the reverence typically reserved for prophets. Considering the depth of his lyrics and ideologies, one can see why. But Bob's vision of the world was forged by a country whose perspective was constructed with an underdog mentality. "Wi likkle but wi tallawah" is a declaration by Jamaicans that they can see the world of paradoxes around them and feel empowered to disrupt them.

To understand more about Jamaica's mentality, you have to look closer at the tiny Caribbean island's history. Prior to 1655, Jamaica was a Spanish colony. Steeped in the slave trade, the Spaniards populated the island almost exclusively with Africans. With only a few native Arawak people and a limited population of Spanish colonists, the island was overwhelmingly African.

After the British defeated the Spanish and took control of the island in 1655, Jamaica saw a large influx of English citizens. Because of the tropical climate and unfamiliar tropical disease, Jamaica's appeal to English colonists waned over time. This created a unique environment where the population had more oppressed Africans than English oppressors.

This population disparity between oppressed and oppressor led to multiple rebellions, and the British struggled to keep control of the entire island. While many of these uprisings were sporadic and uncoordinated, things changed in 1673. That year the first organized revolt of about two hundred slaves created the Leeward Maroons. The frequency and sophistication of revolts increased over the next several years. These intermittent skirmishes culminated in what was called the First Maroon War.

The Maroons, led by Queen Nanny, used advanced military tactics and creative strategies to frustrate their opponents. The English struggled so mightily against Nanny's Maroons on the battlefield that they were forced to sign a treaty. That treaty with the Maroons included freedom and five hundred acres. Nanny had such an impact on Jamaica's history and emancipation that she was declared a national hero in 1975—the only female to receive such a prestigious honor. She and the Maroons were the first Africans in Jamaica to fight for their freedom and win.

Nanny was an absolutely brilliant tactician. She used the terrain, surprise attacks, misdirection, and camouflage. There were even reports of soldiers decreasing their breathing rate to avoid detection in the dense forest. Though outgunned and without formal military training, Nanny brought the British to their knees. She and the Maroons weren't granted freedom. They disagreeably took it. When Marley wrote "Redemption Song," Nanny was already on Jamaica's five-hundred-dollar bill. She was Jamaica's original disruptor.

It's no wonder that Bob Marley told the world to emancipate themselves from mental slavery. Jamaica's perceived slight isn't so perceived after all. After being oppressed by the Spanish and handed to the British, freedom came from conflict. Freedom came from disagreeableness. Freedom came from disruption. Nanny saw the Jamaican Colony paradox, and she refused to accept it. Nanny knew that the truth—the injustice of slavery, genocide, and oppression—was a two-edged sword that cuts sharp.

CHAPTER 17

AN APPLE A DAY

Great success always comes at the risk of enormous failure.

–Winston Churchill

Nanny's ability to see through the oppression paradox is obvious now. But at the time it was a potentially fatal risk—a risk that kept most Jamaicans subdued. Nanny and her fellow Maroons risked their lives for what, paradoxically, they should have had all along. Fortunately for Jamaicans, Nanny's calculated risk paid off. But it wouldn't be a risk unless failing was a real probability.

That's the challenge with disruption. As sexy as it sounds to paint outside the lines, that disagreeable act carries significant risk. That risk is obvious when you're at war with an entire nation that has enslaved your people. But the stakes aren't always so obvious. CNBC's 2018 top disruptors list was full of companies that have become household names, but many others failed to achieve the same notoriety. Disruption is a scary and often ill-fated endeavor. When it works out, it shifts paradigms, but when it fails, it fails.

One of the most promising disruptors identified by CNBC was Nebula. Nebula was ranked thirty-first on CNBC's 2014 list.[83] Like many tech start-up companies, Nebula originated in Mountain View, California. It was one of the many companies that dove headfirst into cloud computing.

Cloud computing revolutionized the tech world. Companies now had the ability to store mass quantities of data in a virtual space rather than physically keeping the data on bulky servers. Before cloud computing, companies would spend millions on supercooled security-laden rooms that housed wall-to-wall computers. By partnering with Nebula, companies looking to house their data virtually could save millions.

Established companies measured their success by earning revenue directly from the products they bring to market. For new companies, the finances are a little different. Most start-up companies carry the burden of debt from starting a business de novo. For them, success is measured by the amount of investment dollars they raise.

As you might expect from their position on this list, Nebula raised millions. Even before it caught CNBC's eye, Nebula was named one of CIO.com's ten hottest cloud companies to watch. As disruptors go, Nebula was more than well positioned to dominate an industry that didn't even exist several years earlier. Or so you would think.

Unfortunately, Nebula declared bankruptcy on April 1, 2015. Nebula faced the risk of disrupting the data-storage convention, and

---

83   Lori Ioannou, "2014 CNBC Disruptor 50: The Most Innovative Start-Ups in Business," CNBC, updated June 17, 2014, https://www.cnbc.com/2014/06/17/2014-cnbc-disruptor-50-the-most-innovative-start-ups-in-business.html.

they failed. They had chosen an appropriate convention to disrupt. They had a high-level leadership team with experience from NASA and Amazon. Nebula didn't fail because of what they did wrong. Mostly, they were doing things the right way. Nebula failed because it was only one of the hundreds of disruptors in the same space that were also doing things the right way.

Nebula wasn't alone. Quirky, an invention platform that connects inventors with companies looking for specialized product inventions, raised over $100 million according to CNBC. They made the CNBC list in both 2014 and 2015. They went bankrupt in 2015—the same year they were selected as the fifteenth top disruptor in the world.[84]

Aereo, a streaming service disruptor and number seven on the disruptor list, is now bankrupt. Blippar was ninth on the 2016 list—bankrupt. And EcoMotors, the twenty-second company on the 2014 list, also went bankrupt. Disruption is downright dangerous! Disruptor deaths are abrupt and surgical, and many dissolve as quickly as they ascend.

Disruptors and disruptive companies tend to burn hot, but many don't burn for long. This reality means that most disruptors are steeped in optimism. For stabilizers, the difference between winning and losing is very narrow. Instead of wowing the crowd by attempting a quad and risking a fall, they focus on perfecting the easier triple salchow. The likelihood of failure far outweighs the potential gain from disruption. And the opposite is true for disruptors.

Disagreeableness is the quality that helps disruptors recognize and disrupt paradoxes. However, disagreeableness isn't enough. To sustain disruption over time requires optimism. Nanny's inability to accept British oppression led to isolated uprisings and revolts. But

---

84 "Meet the 2015 CNBC Disruptor 50 Companies," CNBC, updated February 2, 2016, https://www.cnbc.com/2015/05/12/cnbc-disruptor-50.html.

the sustained leadership necessary to wage a decade-long campaign required optimism.

Yuka Sato won a gold medal in true stabilizer fashion by not making mistakes. She didn't practice until she got it right. Sato practiced until she never got it wrong. The ten-thousand-hour philosophy—the concept that mastery requires ten thousand hours of meaningful work—is about limiting mistakes. Mastery is about getting as close to perfection as possible. Therefore, mastery is also about getting as close to a standard as possible. That's a convention! Mastery is the best way to master painting within the lines.

Disruption is entirely different because there isn't a standard way to disrupt. Painting outside the lines means operating outside the standard, not getting as close as possible to it. Thus, there can't be a standard for a nonstandard method. There can't be a convention to an unconventional process. Good disruptors find those standards and scribble all over them.

Dictionary.com defines optimism as "a disposition or tendency to look on the more favorable side of events or conditions and to expect the most favorable outcome."

Only an optimist would believe that destroying a standard requiring ten thousand hours could ever result in success. It took years of unprofitable futility before Amazon became a financial behemoth. Those futile years, when profitable quarters were few and far between, required a disposition that expected the most favorable outcome despite the quarter-to-quarter mediocrity.

Imagine the optimism needed to oppose the British Empire and commandeer your freedom. Like most disruptors, Nanny had a unique combination of disagreeableness and optimism. By comparison, stabilizers are agreeable, and their goal is to avoid mistakes. These opposites approach the world in two very different ways: one is inspired and hopeful to succeed and the other is preoccupied with avoiding failure.

On October 25, 1974, Marley released the song "Revolution." The song's second line reveals his unique combination of disagreeableness and optimism: "It takes a revolution to make a solution." Bob is advocating for a revolution—a forcible disruption in government and social strata—that leads to a solution.

That juxtaposition, using disagreeableness to yield an optimistic outcome, is the blueprint for disruption. It's Barry O'Shea to billion-dollar CEO. It's oppressed insurgents to free citizens. It's backflips to skating legend. It's a disagreeable act coupled with outcome optimism. Both are required for any successful disruptor, and both are required for greatness.

Common wisdom depicts disruption as an anomaly. However, the universe is more prone to disruption than it is to propagating standards. The second law of thermodynamics seems to support that hypothesis. It states that entropy—defined as a lack of order or predictability—continuously increases.

By this definition, standards and conventions are anomalies, and the universe is compelled to constantly disrupt them. Throughout history, society has been responsible for creating order out of perpetually increasing disorder. Society's structure helps us predict the unpredictable and makes chaos less chaotic.

Disruption, at least from a scientific perspective, is natural. But we have spent millennia creating structures, conventions, and rules to corral that increasing entropy. Of course, some level of structure is necessary in society. Stabilizers are needed in math, science, and even business. The world is full of logical relationships that follow distinct and definitive rules.

The earth's rotation around the sun is consistent. The cosmic relationship between the sun and the earth has followed a predictable course for millions of years. Human hearts have distinct electrical patterns. When those patterns are disrupted, otherwise known as an arrhythmia, the heart's ability to pump blood to the rest of the body is compromised.

Rules are relationships supported by mathematical principles and are very different from conventions. Rules have supporting evidence, like the sun coming up every day for millions of years. Conventions, on the other hand, are relationships that we swear by without supporting evidence. We create them through our groupthink or our consensus or our hubris.

Conventions are relationships that we believe are rules because we haven't taken the time to thoroughly examine our presumptions. Those presumptions were wrong about Stephen Curry. They were wrong about Surya Bonaly. They were wrong about the New York Giants *twice!* And they were wrong about me.

The chasm between stabilizers and disruptors may be somewhat overestimated. While the two have qualitative differences, their differences are more meaningful when you consider the milieu in which they exist. In the midst of a paradox, a disruptor will challenge it. Stabilizers, on the other hand, often reinforce a paradox—even when doing so may result in failure.

Shemar Morrow was an underachieving stabilizer who succumbed to the best-twelve-year-old-in-the-country convention. He was unable to get better faster than the other players were getting better. So Shemar got worse. Shemar was unable to asymptote to what he thought was a standard. He was entropy that was obligated to follow the laws of thermodynamics. If he had disrupted that convention, he would have realized that the best twelve-year-old in the country doesn't always become the best twenty-year-old in the country.

The same is true in business leadership. Different leadership styles resonate with various stages of a company's life cycle. Small start-up companies tend to do better with disruptive leaders. Larger, slow-moving, and older companies tend to do better with stabilizers. While most companies prefer one type of leader over another, a few companies cycle between disruptors and stabilizers. One of those is Apple.

Apple disrupted the programming world when its Apple I desktop computer went on sale in 1976 for $666. This marked the beginning of Apple's disruption. Steve Jobs and Steve Wozniak disrupted a paradox. Computers at that time were expensive, bulky, and reserved for businesses and the rich. Jobs and Wozniak believed that the power of the computer belonged to the individual. During an interview in the May 1977 issue of *Byte* magazine, Wozniak described the purpose of his second iteration of the Apple computer: "To me, a personal computer should be small, reliable, convenient to use, and inexpensive."[85]

This disagreeable statement conflicted with the computing standard of the time. Jobs and Wozniak did what most disruptive leaders do. They disrupted a convention within a paradox—and, by doing so, created an entirely new business category. This is your typical start-up story: founders who identify an area to disrupt and optimistically set out to change the world. The optimism of Apple's founders was so high that they both dropped out of their respective colleges. And no, they didn't attend Ivy League schools.

Apple was one of the best-known disruptive start-ups in history. It wasn't the first, but Apple has become the embodiment of the start-it-in-your-garage tech company. Apple's disruptive foundation was

---

85 Stephen Wozniak, "The Apple-II," *Byte*, May 1977, 34.

amplified even further by its disruptor founders. With that combination, Apple took off. The small, private company was so successful that it went public in December 1980. When their IPO opened at $22 per share, investor exuberance rivaled the energy of the Nagano crowd after Surya's backflip. After the first day of trading, Apple's market capitalization—the aggregate market value of a company—was almost $1.8 billion.

Market scrutiny of a public company is far different from that of a private one. Public companies have investors who expect returns. After all, that's why investors invest. After Apple's early disruptor success, the company entered a new phase of its life cycle. Competitors such as IBM, Atari, and Amiga ventured into the personal computing space, forcing Apple to compete rather than disrupt.

Instead of finding new business conventions to disrupt, Apple altered its course to focus on getting better faster than its competitors were getting better—so they didn't get worse. This approach initially returned reasonable dividends to the horde of hungry investors. However, a company founded on disruption quickly lost ground to better stabilizers. The market created new lines that publicly traded companies had to make sure that they painted between. And Apple, whose compulsion was to change the world through disruption, was competing as a stabilizer. They were suffering from the same plight as Shemar.

After several difficult years, Apple returned to their disruptive ways. They brought back Steve Jobs, who had been ousted during their stabilizer era. How did Apple recover? They returned to the principles they were founded on. They disrupted the music industry with the iPod and created a whole new market with the iPad. The new Apple was so disruptive it cannibalized its own iPod business and replaced it by launching the iPhone. They also continued to add new features to the iPhone that disrupted several other spaces. In 2022 Apple was the seventh-largest company in the world.

Apple's disruptive persona deepened with Steve Jobs's return. In the same vein as Wozniak's intent to change the personal computing space, the second iteration of Apple attempted to do the same in the personal device space. Instead of making a cheaper and more convenient personal computer for the desktop, they placed desktop computing functions directly in the consumer's hands. In the process Apple all but destroyed several long-standing personal device industries, including cameras, calculators, personal data assistants, music players, and countless others.

Apple's original mindset was to change the world and assume the revenue would follow. That mindset created two of the most disruptive developments in their history. Apple used their phone—something individuals always had with them—as a platform to bring other functions to the consumer. Instead of being forced to release a new hardware version every time a new software application was released, they allowed other software companies to create applications for their iPhones. This made the iPhone a great calculator, camera, and MP3 player—and it also made the iPhone a platform for developers to share iOS applications with the world. This made the iPhone something you bought to engage with Apple, but it also made the iPhone something you bought to engage with almost anybody else.

Apple went from disruptor to stabilizer and back to disruptor again. Who they were in the business environment was a function of who led them. They built a company around disruption but briefly forgot they needed a disruptive leader to maintain that approach. Sadly, Steve Jobs died in 2011 from a rare form of pancreatic cancer. Under Tim Cook, Apple's new CEO and Steve Jobs's protégé, Apple continues to disrupt. As the personal device industry gets increasingly competitive, Apple will find it increasingly challenging to find new conventions to disrupt.

As is typical of disruptor-stabilizer cycles, Apple's disruption may soon reach an inflection point. From December 2021 to December 2022, Apple brought in almost $66 billion from iPhone sales, which represents over half of its total revenues.[86] According to Counterpoint, Apple's share of the smartphone business is approximately 16 percent, second only to Samsung.[87] Competing with Samsung, Google, and others to win the personal phone market could plunge Apple into another stabilizer phase. Over the next several years, the challenge will be to continue to disrupt rather than try to make the iPhone better faster than its competitors are getting better—so that it doesn't get worse.

The good news for Apple is that they continue to disrupt in other areas. In that same fiscal year, Apple brought in $13.5 billion from wearables, including earphones and watches. They also earned $20.8 billion from music streaming and other subscription services. And what about Apple's desktop? Only $7.7 billion in revenue came from Apple I's latest descendant—the iMac. Apple's lowest revenue comes from the first product it disrupted the market with. Apple's propensity for disruption is so powerful that it disrupted its own disruption.[88] Now that's disruptive!

Like Nanny and Surya, Apple succeeded by taking significant risks. Disrupting an industry you've created could've been cataclysmic.

---

86 Mike Wuerthele, "Notes of Interest from Apple's Q4 2021 and Annual Earnings Report," AppleInsider, October 28, 2021, https://appleinsider.com/articles/21/10/28/notes-of-interest-from-apples-q4-2021-and-annual-earnings-report.

87 "Apple iPhone Market Share: Quarterly," Counterpoint Quarterly, May 29, 2024, https://www.counterpointresearch.com/insights/apple-iphone-market-share-quarter/.

88 Counterpoint Quarterly, "Apple iPhone Market Share: Quarterly."

CHAPTER 17

Identifying paradoxes is challenging enough, but shouldering the risk necessary to act is much harder. Marley's album *Exodus* was recorded in London during his self-imposed exile from Jamaica and during a period of significant risk. His popularity made him a living legend, but that popularity also attracted its share of political conflict.

Marley's popularity in Jamaica reached its height at the same time as Jamaica's political conflict. Michael Manley, who led the socialist People's National Party, and Edward Seaga, who headed the more conservative Jamaica Labour Party, were at the center of this conflict. During this volatile period between 1972 and 1992, Michael Manley and Edward Seaga would alternately rule Jamaica: Manley from 1972 to 1980, Seaga from 1980 to 1989, and then Manley again from 1989 to 1992.

To gain an advantage, Manley and Seaga hired gang members mostly to protect themselves and partly to support their causes. The political conflict and raging gang wars became indistinguishable. Marley was caught in the political cross fire. By neither supporting nor condemning either party, he became a target for both. While each candidate denied any relationship with Jamaica's gangs, it was well known that many gangs had political allegiances.

In December 1976 the conflict found its way into Marley's home. Marley, his manager, and his wife were all shot that night. The bullet grazed his chest and hit him in the arm. His wife and manager were more seriously hurt, though all fully recovered.

Many believe that the attempt on Marley's life was an effort by the Seaga's camp to dissuade him from participating in "Smile Jamaica," which was a free concert organized by Michael Manley. Two days after the attempt, Marley defiantly performed the concert in front of eighty thousand people. When asked why he still did the concert, Marley told reporters, "The people who are trying to make this world worse aren't taking a day off. How can I?"[89]

In 1978 Marley did it again. He decided to stage a "One Love Peace Concert" to subdue the warring factions. He was bold enough to invite Manley and Seaga on stage and encouraged them to shake hands. With over thirty-two thousand spectators, it was one of the most monumental moments in Jamaican history. Marley, who left Jamaica after a politically motivated assassination attempt on his life because he was going to perform in a peace concert, went back to Jamaica to perform in a peace concert to bring two political factions together. Disagreeable and optimistic, that's the definition of Bob Marley. That's the definition of a disruptor.

Marley risked his life to disrupt Jamaica's political dissonance. What success could be worth such an enormous risk? Marley himself sums it up: "Well, my life no important to me, other people life important. My life is only important if me can help plenty people. If my life is just for me and my own security, then me no want it. My life is for people. That's the way me is."[90]

---

89 John Kruth, "A Look Back at Bob Marley Masterpiece, 'Exodus,'" *American Songwriter*, accessed June 24, 2024, https://americansongwriter.com/exodus-by-bob-marley/.

90 Midnight Raver, "Bob Marley Interviewed by Bruce Morrow (NBC News), NYC, March 16, 1978," April 13, 2017, YouTube, https://www.youtube.com/watch?v=zstEAjhH0yc.

CHAPTER 18

Them Want to See the Truth

> *We will be relentless in our pursuit of perfection. We won't ever be perfect—but in the process we will achieve greatness.*
>
> —Vince Lombardi

The odd combination of disagreeableness and optimism is a hallmark of disruptors. Their disagreeableness makes them particularly sensitive to paradoxes, and their optimism enables them to see uncommon outcomes to long-standing conventions. These attributes are consistent, but there is at least one more consistent quality. Vince Lombardi described the quality indirectly. A relentless pursuit of perfection combined with the understanding that perfection is impossible describes an asymptote.

Do you remember your high school math? An asymptote is a line that approaches a curve and grows infinitely closer without ever actually touching that curve. Stabilizers pursue perfection like asymptotes. They work hard to get as close to perfection as possible. For stabilizers, winners and losers are determined by how close a performance comes to perfection. ISU judging standards, as an example, are based on how close a performance is to skating perfection.

Disruptors, on the other hand, pursue perfection to achieve greatness. See the subtle difference? For stabilizers, excellence is a goal. For disruptors, pursuing excellence is a path to something greater. That's why Surya was compelled to keep raising the bar. The judges judged her based on her asymptote to excellence rather than the greatness she was trying to achieve. It's a subtle but not-so-subtle difference.

Trish Novicio, in a Yahoo Finance article from February 17, 2021, describes the qualities of serial entrepreneurs as individuals who disrupt and disrupt and disrupt.[91] They jump headfirst into building companies that focus on disrupting other companies. Serial disruptors aren't always successful. When they fail, they pick themselves up, recover, and go off to the next start-up. As the name implies, serial disruptors are perpetually focused on the next disruptive opportunity. That try-try-again mindset makes sense when they fail, but serial entrepreneurs continue to create new companies even when they *succeed*.

Steve Jobs's time away from Apple wasn't spent reveling in his former disruptive brilliance. His compulsive disruption continued. Jobs created NeXT, an operating system company that sold to Apple for over $500 million. Jobs also bought a small animation company for $5 million and sold it for $7 billion. That company was Pixar. Steve Jobs succeeded after succeeding, and this road of serial disruptive success isn't as uncommon as one might think.

---

[91] Trish Novicio, "Top 15 Serial Entrepreneurs in the World," Yahoo Finance, February 17, 2021, https://finance.yahoo.com/news/top-15-serial-entrepreneurs-world-181004627.html?guccounter=2.

CHAPTER 18

The National Bureau of Economic Research released a paper titled "Skill vs. Luck in Entrepreneurship and Venture Capital: Evidence from Serial Entrepreneurs."[92] After studying serial entrepreneurs, the authors concluded, "Our results indicate that skill is an important determinant of success for entrepreneurial startups. Successful serial entrepreneurs are more likely to replicate the success of their past companies than either single venture entrepreneurs or serial entrepreneurs who failed in their prior venture." So serial entrepreneurs don't try-try-again. They succeed and succeed again.

The authors found that serial entrepreneurs who win continue to win. They identified particular entrepreneurial skills that make some serial entrepreneurs more successful than others. The article continues describing this unique type of disruptor. "While our paper identifies entrepreneurial skill, it does not distinguish exactly what the critical entrepreneurial skill is." That said, if we look closely, we can postulate that certain skills matter more than others. Disagreeableness and optimism are essential for entry into the disruption game. Meaning those qualities are requisite to start the disruptive process. However, those qualities aren't enough to sustain disruption.

Originally copublished with Harvard University, the National Bureau paper also found that serial entrepreneurs "exhibit persistence in selecting the right industry and time to start new ventures." This also describes Nanny, Surya, Marley, and many of the disruptors we've discussed thus far. Nanny and the Maroons used guerrilla tactics against an oppressive force that was far more powerful. Surya risked her chance at Olympic gold to raise the bar and pursue greatness. After being shot, Marley returned to Jamaica to bring two warring

---

92 Paul Gompers et al., "Skill vs. Luck in Entrepreneurship and Venture Capital: Evidence from Serial Entrepreneurs," National Bureau of Economic Research, October 2006, http://www.nber.org/papers/w12592.

LESS THAN ONE PERCENT

political factions together and unite Jamaica. While the authors describe serial entrepreneurs as persistent, they're better described by the term "relentless."

Dictionary.com defines relentless as "not easing or slackening; maintaining speed, vigor and unyieldingly severe, strict, or harsh." For a minute, think of what an odd combination of traits disruptors have: optimism sandwiched between disagreeableness and unyielding relentlessness. In the business world, that combination of qualities takes fledgling start-ups to multibillion-dollar companies. At first glance, relentless disagreeableness and the optimism to succeed aren't exactly a combination that you would expect to be successful. But as we've seen before, disruptors aren't pursuing success. They're pursuing something far more significant.

On January 21, 2015, one of the greatest NBA players of all time was doing what he always does: dominating on the court. Kobe Bryant's Lakers were up by four points against the New Orleans Pelicans. Kobe drove along the baseline and jumped in the air from just under the basket. Two players converged to block his view of the rim. Just before he landed and to avoid being blocked, Kobe bounced the ball off the back of the player next to him—essentially passing the ball to himself. He turned, faded, and made the miraculous shot. The play was downright ridiculous.

With four minutes left in the third quarter and the Lakers down by two, Kobe drove from the right baseline and dunked the ball to put the Lakers up by one point. About halfway down the court, he grabbed his right shoulder. Unfortunately, he had just torn his rotator cuff. Kobe went to the bench, and the training staff wrapped his shoulder in ice. Everyone thought he was done for the night—everyone except Kobe Bryant.

CHAPTER 18

In the fourth quarter, he took the wrap off and went back into the game. No one knew the extent of the injury until Kobe could barely move his arm. He had almost no range of motion in the injured right shoulder, which was his dominant side. Then he went to his patented mid-post, dribbled twice, and took a turnaround jump shot. *Swish.* It was a classic Kobe Bryant move, except that he shot the ball with his left hand. He shot the ball with his nondominant hand.

That nonchalant moment truly described Kobe Bryant. Kobe was beyond talented, but that wasn't what made him the greatest of all time. Kobe was relentless. Players rarely shoot jump shots with their nondominant hands. Players almost never shoot jump shots with their nondominant hand, when the game is on the line. Kobe was unyieldingly severe. The show must go on.

This wasn't the only time Kobe's relentlessness declared itself. A few years earlier, with just over six minutes left in the game, Kobe drove toward the basket and spun. As he spun and got fouled, his leg gave out, and he almost fell. Kobe grabbed his leg in pain and limped to half-court. He massaged his lower leg and was bent over in obvious pain. Of course, he continued to play.

Later in that game, Kobe made an explosive move to the basket. As soon as he made his move, he crumpled to the ground. This time he could hardly put any weight on his leg and stayed down. It took him a few minutes to stand up and limp to the free throw line. He made two free throws to tie the game and hobbled off the court with a third-degree Achilles tendon rupture.

Kobe built a career based on relentlessness, the same quality that disruptors and serial entrepreneurs use to battle conventions. If Surya had just stopped attempting quads and backflips, she might have avoided placing second by the slimmest of margins. Marley could have written a song about peace rather than flying to Jamaica and bringing two mortal enemies together. But their relentlessness made their disruption "unyieldingly severe." Relentlessness makes disruption a compulsion.

In her Yahoo Finance article, Novicio also identified another quality that helped serial entrepreneurs succeed time and time again: "While chasing success has always been the goal for many business founders, serial entrepreneurs are anti-fragile: they gain from failure." Developed by Nassim Nicholas Taleb, antifragility is a term that refers to the relative resilience of a company or individual.

An antifragile company has a paradoxical reaction to negative impacts. Volatility, setbacks, failures, stressors, and other factors that would typically limit a company's performance paradoxically *enhance* an antifragile company's performance. Individuals can also be antifragile, and Novicio argues that serial entrepreneurs succeed because of this quality.

Many make the inappropriate assumption that high success rates mean these serial entrepreneurs don't experience failure. Have you heard of the Apple Lisa? The Lisa desktop computer was another Steve Jobs creation, and it was an absolute failure. While the Macintosh targeted personal users, the Lisa was marketed to businesses. It was full of innovative technology and sold for a whopping $10,000 in 1983—definitely not consistent with his computer-for-all price point of the aforementioned Mac. From a product perspective, the Lisa was sluggish because of the high demand on the central processing unit. The market responded in kind, with only ten thousand units sold in two years. The Lisa was a bust.

The Lisa wasn't Jobs's only failure. Macintosh TV and the Power Mac G4 Cube were also colossal failures. In the case of the antifragile, failures accelerate the next disruption. Surya Bonaly never won on the national stage. Though she had multiple French and European championships, when it came to a world title, she never won! If attempting quads and focusing on athleticism over style wasn't successful, why wouldn't she change her focus? Why would she culminate her amateur career with history's most audacious and controversial jump? It was because of her antifragility.

Surya's multiple losses accelerated her disruption. Instead of curbing her disruptive tendencies, she disrupted more! She wasn't dissuaded by the skating version of the Apple Lisa. That's the disruptive paradox. The judges penalized her because she pushed the envelope—which only increased her propensity to disrupt, which, in turn, increased the likelihood of being penalized.

Surya was skating's equivalent of a serial entrepreneur. Failure didn't dissuade her. It emboldened her. That resolve was evident in the Netflix special *Losers*. "If I didn't win or finish at the top, I probably didn't do enough," we hear Surya say. "My only goal was I need to do more than anyone else."

The mixture of disagreeableness, optimism, relentlessness, and antifragility is fundamental to true disruptors. These traits don't exist to the exclusion of others, but they're present in all disruptors in some combination. This unique makeup allows them to identify paradoxes and disrupt the conventions buried beneath them. Which begs the question, Can others, who aren't identified as disruptors, do the same? The answer is, well, complicated.

Paradoxes and conventions are obvious when you have evidence and data. However, the data and evidence aren't always so obvious. While living in a paradox, one can only see the paradox. The convention is so strong that seeing the truth is extremely difficult. The skills and qualities that made Steph Curry a phenom in the NBA are the same skills and qualities that made him a phenom in college, which are the same skills and qualities that earned him the 256th ranking in the class of 2006.

Of the hundreds of high school evaluators in 2006, wasn't there even one disruptor? Why was no one disagreeable enough to uncover the developing Steph Curry paradox? Why weren't any of the judges as excited as the crowd to see Surya's once-in-a-generation maneuver? Why didn't NASA listen to Roger Boisjoly?

Unfortunately, broad groupthink inhibits disruption, and overcoming that inhibition requires courage. Not one evaluator had the courage to disprove the convention building around Stephen Curry. Bob McKillop didn't believe the Stephen Curry convention because he had the courage to look at basketball recruits differently.

Do you remember McKillop's comments about Steph Curry?

> He played in one of the auxiliary gyms, not the main gym…. And he was awful. He threw the ball into the stands, he dropped passes, he dribbled off his foot, he missed shots. But never once during that game did he blame an official, or point a finger at a teammate. He was always cheering from the bench, he looked in his coach's eyes, and he never flinched. That stuck with me.

As a recruiter, McKillop was a disruptor. He didn't mention the conventional qualities that make recruiters drool, such as athleticism, skills, talent, or upside.

Coach McKillop wasn't interested in getting a player that the other teams were trying to get—so he could get better faster than other teams were getting better. He was interested in finding greatness, which is profoundly different from finding a recruit who's slightly more athletic or shoots a slightly higher percentage. Most college coaches are recruiting to an asymptote. As a result they find players closer who are better than other players, but they rarely find transcendent players.

It isn't just recruiting. Chaos is terrifying, and conventions add structure to a universe of ever-increasing entropy. Following conventions is safe and provides a level of stability. That stability makes the stabilizer pathway much more appealing to so many. In a 1979 interview with Dylan Taite in New Zealand, Bob Marley unknowingly described society's struggle with the need for conventions: "Every day them get up. Them look on the TV. Them read the newspaper. Them want to see the truth, but them can't see the truth. Because the truth will not be found there."[93]

Marley was referring to a convention's ability to obscure the truth. Those paradoxes and conventions are created by society's standards, which Marley believed are distributed through newspapers and television. He believed most people wanted to see the truth, but they couldn't. The same is true with paradoxes. We all want the truth, but the truth is difficult to attain unless we commit to looking at things differently. And maybe even that isn't enough. If we genuinely want to see the truth, we must embody the characteristics of those who relentlessly seek it.

---

93   Rasta Vibration, "Bob Marley—1979 Interview in New Zealand," June 22, 2012, YouTube, https://www.youtube.com/watch?v=xiaZJdOqHw0.

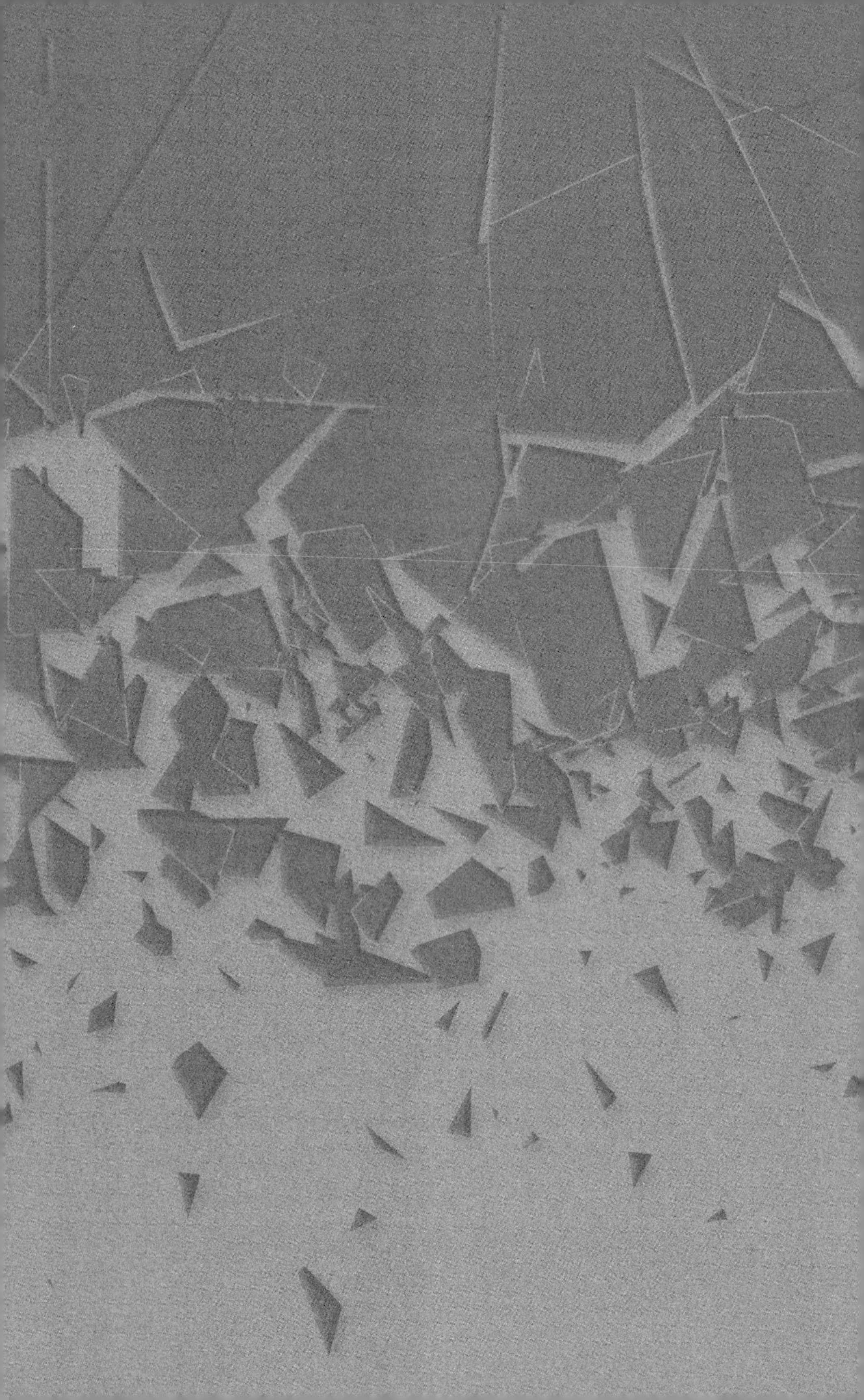

CHAPTER 19

NASSAU AND MACAO

He will wipe away every tear from their eyes, and death shall be no more, neither shall there be mourning, nor crying, nor pain anymore, for the former things have passed away.

–Revelation 21:4 (English Standard Version)

I heard him running down the hall to see his grandmother who had just arrived. He had been in bed all night. I can't remember when he didn't sleep in the bed with us. He was on his fourth or fifth drug cocktail. With every change, there was hope.

I was frustrated the night before. He couldn't remember his prayers but could repeat my words if I prompted him. "Gentle Jesus, meek and mild. Look upon a little child. Make me good. O Lord, I pray—Amen." He couldn't finish, so I finished for him.

I teared up each time he said the words. They came out slowly, like someone who was searching for the words. I worked all night and crawled into bed, careful not to wake him up. As long as he was asleep, he did fine. It was the waking hours that caused terror.

He was so happy to see his grandmother. Usually, I would run right behind him. The term "helicopter parent" would fall woefully short of where I was at that time. I figured this was as good a time as any. Eventually, we would have to cut the tether. The constant watching and worrying was taking its toll on all of us.

I don't often get tired, but that day I was exhausted. I felt and looked horrible. My coworkers tolerated me because they knew what I was going through. I was disheveled and making mistakes. I don't make mistakes. I hated to sleep, but emotional fatigue made me physically and mentally weak. For a few minutes, I was going to try to get a little rest. And then I heard it.

It's still hard to describe the sound. When I heard it, almost a year ago, it was like nothing I've ever heard before. And now it's something I'd rather not hear ever again. It was a cross between a dog's yelp, a seal's bark, and a pig's squeal. When you're tired and anxious and on edge, you sometimes hear the sound even when you don't hear the sound, especially when the line between awake and asleep isn't much of a line at all.

I jumped out of bed and sprinted to where I thought the sound came from. He was down the hall about twenty feet from me, lying on the ground. His arms and legs were contracting and extending rapidly. His teeth were clenched. He was on his back with frothy saliva leaking from both sides of his mouth.

I slid next to him like a baseball player sliding into home plate. It felt like I was sliding forever. I put my hands under his head to stop it from hitting the floor. I screamed for help. Everyone else came running to us—my wife, his grandma, my daughter, and her Scary Giraffe.

CHAPTER 19

He was seizing! He was having another generalized tonic-clonic seizure. At this point we had our family seizure response down. Someone would run and get the oxygen and the pulse oximeter to ensure he was adequately oxygenating. We had a medicine called a benzodiazepine that we placed in his mouth to stop the seizure. We tried one dose, then another. He kept seizing. This was the longest seizure he had ever had. I can't recall how long it was, but it felt like hours.

We all looked at each other. We had to take him to the hospital. We put him in the back seat of the car with an oxygen mask over his face. He was still seizing. I screeched out of the garage and careened through the neighborhood. At one point I was driving a hundred miles an hour. He was still seizing. It was his longest seizure ever. His lips were blue. I was driving erratically, barely missing oncoming cars. I screeched into the emergency department parking lot, threw my son over my shoulder, and ran inside.

They put him in a bed and hooked everything up to him. He was still seizing. The emergency room staff started getting frantic. They kept giving him medications, and he wouldn't stop. I asked them to put a tube in his throat to help him breathe, which I knew was a common practice to prevent deoxygenation. He was still seizing.

The staff decided to call the children's hospital and urgently called an ambulance to take him to see the specialists there. They gave him some more meds. He kept seizing. They drove to the children's hospital about fifteen minutes away. His mom rode with him in the ambulance, and I sped to the hospital in the car and got there before the ambulance arrived. I called my wife. He was still seizing.

We were put in one of the emergency room's intensive units. While the doctor questioned us, the team continued giving him medications. Nothing was working, and that was the moment I decided to take matters into my own hands. As an emergency physician, I knew what needed to be done. I ripped open a respiratory cart and gathered the materials necessary to intubate him, inserting a tube into his throat to help him breathe. Sweating and crying, I screamed at the physician and nurses to get out of my way. He was still seizing.

I remember that moment like it was yesterday. I thought he was going to die. My firstborn son was going to die, and nobody was helping him. I knew how to save him if they would just get out of my way! I was so angry and scared and sad. At that point they called security. I was so out of control.

It was a standoff, and just when it was about to get even worse, she walked up to me and hugged me—an administrator who had worked at my hospital was now the head of the children's hospital. I was sweaty, dirty, angry, and crying. She hugged me, and he stopped seizing.

At that moment a calm came over me. Everything went away, and somehow even the seizure went away too. That moment wiped away every tear from my eye. There was no more mourning, crying, or pain—the seizures had passed. This moment was my revelation.

Cambridge Dictionary defines revelation as "the act of making something known that was secret." The word "revelation" originated from the Greek word *apokalyptein*, which means to uncover, disclose, or reveal. That experience with my son disrupted almost everything I thought I knew about the conventions of life.

That moment of clarity, when a paradox and its associated conventions are first disrupted, is calming. That moment is the moment when Surya Bonaly landed her first backflip, when Nanny negotiated her freedom from the British, and when Stephen Curry walked across the stage on draft night. This is the truth that Bob Marley discussed in his interview. That pursuit of truth is why we must dissect paradoxes, determine how they work, and uncover the truths they hide. That

CHAPTER 19

clarity allows us to differentiate the transparent truth of rules from the more opaque conventions that live within paradoxes.

The rules we live by aren't invalidated by the presence of paradoxes. Their presence should enhance our understanding of the truth. Their presence doesn't mean we throw out all the rules; breaking a rule is still breaking a rule. At the same time, breaking a convention is breaking a rule that should've never been a rule at all. The difference is the validity of the hypothesis.

If evidence supports a statement, it's appropriate to remain a rule. But if the evidence is inconsistent to support a statement or answer a question, it's likely a paradox. Differentiating between a paradox and a rule is difficult enough for those who can root out the subtle distinctions. But for most, it's as muddy as a dirt road on a rainy day.

Unfortunately, that difference isn't always easy to see. Our Ivy League paradox exposed the relationship between Ivy League education and top CEOs. As a financial investment, the Ivy League didn't necessarily yield the best CEO return. The assumption that spending more on education guarantees a commensurate return is a convention.

Do the same rules apply to elementary and secondary education? Based on the Ivy League convention, increasing financial investment in primary and secondary education shouldn't necessarily result in improved learning. In most states, public education investment is driven by tax revenues, and most of those tax dollars come from real estate. In short, your local public school will receive more money if you live in an affluent neighborhood. To this end, let's look at the wealthiest counties in New York.[94]

---

94 "Per Capita Personal Income by County, Annual: New York," Federal Reserve Economic Data, Federal Reserve Bank of St. Louis, accessed June 26, 2024, https://fred.stlouisfed.org/release/tables?eid=267974&rid=175.

Rank	County	Per Capita Income	Median Family Income	Population	Number of Households
1	New York County	$111,386	$75,629	1,585,873	763,846
2	Westchester	$73,159	$100,863	949,113	347,232
3	Nassau	$41,387	$107,934	1,339,532	448,528
4	Putnam	$37,915	$101,576	99,710	35,041
5	Suffolk	$35,755	$96,220	1,493,350	499,922
6	Rockland	$34,304	$96,836	311,687	99,242
7	Saratoga	$32,186	$81,251	219,607	88,296
8	Columbia	$31,844	$69,132	63,096	25,906
9	Dutchess	$31,642	$83,599	297,488	107,965
10	Albany	$30,863	$76,159	304,204	126,251

These are the most expensive counties in the state of New York. The high incomes in these areas support even higher home prices, which generate more dollars for many young minds. New York has sixty-two counties, and the difference between the richest and poorest is colossal. New York County's per capita income of $111,386 starkly contrasts Bronx County at only $17,575.

How does this income disparity affect education? To determine the impact of tax revenue on school performance, we have to find a way to evaluate how a school is performing. The best way to find out how the school is performing is to test the students. While many schools have different curricula and emphasize various aspects of learning, they all have consistent expectations around math and

English education. Testing allows us to compare schools based on agreed-upon standards. So let's do that comparison, looking again at New York counties and student proficiency in both math and English Language Arts (ELA).[95]

School District	New York County	ELA rank*	% Proficient ELA	Math Rank	% Proficient in Math
Bronxville	Westchester	1	89%	1	88%
Jericho	Nassau	2	88%	2	87%
Scarsdale	Westchester	3	85%	2	87%
East Williston	Nassau	4	83%	2	87%
Herricks	Nassau	4	83%	5	85%
North Shore	Nassau	15	78%	5	85%
Manhasset	Nassau	6	82%	7	82%
Byram Hills	Westchester	13	79%	7	82%
Great Neck	Nassau	12	80%	9	81%
Rye City	Westchester	6	82%	10	80%
Bronxville	Westchester	1	89%	1	88%

When we analyze this data, a consistent pattern emerges. Bronxville and Scarsdale scored first and third in math proficiency. This is calculated by the number of students above the proficiency standard

---

[95] Elizabeth Doran and Kevin Tampone, "2023 NY School Test Scores: Search New English, Math Results for Every District," CNY Schools & Colleges, updated December 15, 2023, https://www.syracuse.com/schools/2023/12/2023-ny-school-test-scores-search-new-english-math-results-for-every-district.html.

divided by the total number of students in the district. Jericho and East Williston follow at second and fourth, respectively. When we look closely at the top eleven school districts by math score, we'll see that all these top districts fall into two counties.

Yes! The top eleven school districts fall into two counties—Westchester and Nassau. These two counties are the second and third wealthiest counties in the state. This relationship flies in the face of the Ivy League paradox. In the case of New York City public schools, the more affluent the county, the better the math performance. In one case, spending more money on education doesn't necessarily lead to success. In the other, spending more comes with a near guarantee of success. How can both scenarios be true?

On the surface, this conflict between learning and financial funding appears irreconcilable. This is why human beings struggle to discern the difference between rules and conventions. If we aren't careful, we might assume that spending more on elementary and secondary school students has the same mediocre effect as spending more on college students. We could go further and postulate that becoming a CEO—a position requiring considerable math and language proficiency—requires a more expensive education. And, of course, we'd be wrong.

Paradoxes don't exist because of what we know. Paradoxes exist because we often refuse to acknowledge what we don't know. In the case of CEOs, we know that education is essential. What's less obvious is how other factors play into the development of CEOs.

Entrepreneurship, leadership, and many other qualities are also necessary to pursue such a career. This is a common mistake, making a correlation between two seemingly similar relationships without fully understanding all the variables and how they relate. Unfortunately, it gets even more complicated.

CHAPTER 19

School districts in wealthy counties often celebrate their performance. Since they spend more per student, they attribute their performance to lower student-to-teacher ratios, more effective initiatives, and better programs. While this may be true, there are also other possible explanations. Students who live in wealthier counties have better access to resources. They also are less likely to be challenged by housing or food insecurities.

The school proficiency paradox follows a completely circular pattern. Wealthier people, who have more resources, move to wealthier counties with higher tax revenues, so those communities can spend more to educate children who have more resources. Poorer counties with poorer students, who will likely require more resources, attend schools with lower tax revenues that spend less per student. Do wealthier school districts do better because they're able to teach more effectively because they have more resources? Or do wealthier school districts do well because they have wealthier students, and wealthier families, who have more resources? Those answers require revelation.

In New York and many other states that use the same tax-based school funding methodology, students with more resources receive more resources from schools with more resources. The opposite is also true. Students with fewer resources receive fewer resources from schools with fewer resources. This methodology for school funding doesn't just create a dichotomy between poor and wealthy students. It deepens it.

America's wealth gap is further compounded by an education gap. This is the truth that Bob Marley was referring to: "There's a force fighting against, not just the music but the truth. Yeah, because sometime the truth is like a two-edged sword. You know, it cut sharp.

That mean plenty people don't like hear the truth. Because plenty people find themselves feeling guilty. So the truth is an offense."[96]

The current education convention is a two-edged sword. The truth that Marley refers to is how the world should be instead of how the world is. This convention that continues to widen the gap between those who have and those who don't have must be disrupted. The revelation that cuts sharp is that students with fewer resources actually need more resources to be proficient. In that model, the gap between school districts narrows, but the overall proficiency of the entire state improves. Because people find themselves feeling guilty, it's easier to ignore this unique challenge rather than acknowledge that an entire educational system needs to be disrupted.

There's even more evidence that the educational funding methodology is inadequate. In 2015 the Pew Research Center published math scores based on the International Student Assessment. Like math scores in New York, students worldwide were evaluated on science and reading proficiency.[97]

---

96 metisrastaman, "Bob Marley Interview 1979," August 12, 2011, YouTube, https://www.youtube.com/watch?v=D10R8ZYHkNM&feature=youtu.be.

97 Drew Desilver, "US Students' Academic Achievement Still Lags That of Their Peers in Many Other Countries," Pew Research Center, February 15, 2017, https://www.pewresearch.org/short-reads/2017/02/15/u-s-students-internationally-math-science/.

CHAPTER 19

Rank	Country	Math Score
1	Singapore	564
2	Hong Kong	548
3	Macao	544
4	Taiwan	542
5	Japan	532
6	South Korea	524
7	Switzerland	521
8	Estonia	520
9	Canada	516
10	Netherlands	512
11	Finland	511
12	Denmark	511
13	Slovenia	510
14	Belgium	507
15	Germany	506
16	Ireland	504
17	Poland	504
18	Norway	502
19	Austria	497
20	New Zealand	495
21	Vietnam	495
22	Australia	494
23	Sweden	494
24	Russia	494
25	France	493
26	United Kingdom	492
27	Portugal	492
28	Czech Republic	492
29	Italy	490
30	OECD Average	490
31	Iceland	488
32	Spain	486
33	Luxembourg	486
34	Latvia	482
35	Malta	479
36	Lithuania	478
37	Hungary	477
38	Slovakia	475
39	*United States*	*470*
40	Israel	470

The United States has the world's highest GDP—the total value of goods produced and services provided in a country during one year. Though there are several ways to measure a country's wealth, GDP is a reasonable way to measure overall economic success. Education, healthcare, transportation, and a host of other public services that support a country's population are directly related to the country's financial resources. National education shouldn't be any different. A higher GDP should result in more resources for students, which, in turn, should improve performance.

Although the United States has the world's highest GDP, its math scores barely crack the top forty. In fact, the United States is significantly below the Organisation for Economic Co-operation and Development average.[98] Just above the United States is Malta, whose GDP ranks 132nd globally. Students from Macao, a tiny island nation of just 680,000 people, rank third on this prestigious list. To put things in perspective, Macao's GDP is $47 billion compared with America's whopping $25 trillion![99] So by GDP, the United States is 632 times wealthier than Macao.

This relationship between money and education is confusing. In the case of the Ivy League, an expensive education doesn't always yield chief executive outcomes. That relationship reverses in New York State, where the wealth of a school district is directly proportional to outcomes in math.

Finally, that relationship reverses again when we focus on national wealth and its relationship with national math scores. Three entirely

---

98 "Comparing Countries' and Economies' Performance in Mathematics," PISA 2022 Results, Organisation for Economic Co-operation and Development, https://www.oecd.org/pisa/OECD_2022_PISA_Results_Comparing%20countries'%20and%20economies'%20performance%20in%20mathematics.pdf.

99 C. Textor, "Gross Domestic Product (GDP) at Current Prices of Macao from 2000 to 2023 with Forecasts Until 2029," Statista, April 17, 2024, https://www.statista.com/statistics/319473/macau-gross-domestic-product/.

CHAPTER 19

different relationships between money and education scores exist simultaneously. This is the type of confusion that makes finding Bob Marley's truth so difficult.

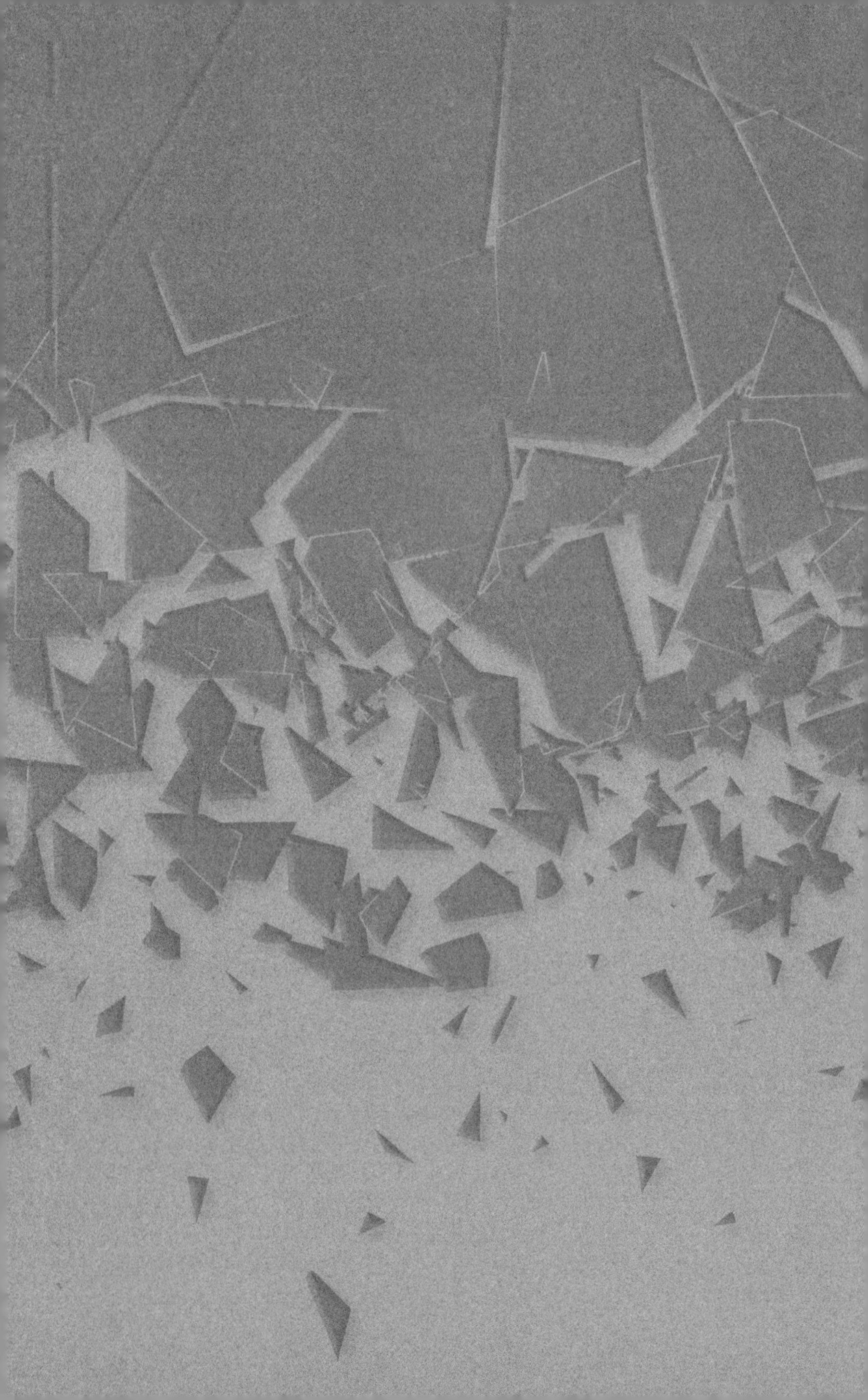

CHAPTER 20

Deception

Our first impressions are generated by our experiences and our environment, which means that we can change our first impressions ... by changing the experiences that comprise those impressions.

–Malcolm Gladwell

Everybody was hustling through the terminal. That's the grind of city life. Everybody is in a hurry. That day-to-day grind, bustling through the gauntlet of public transportation, makes it difficult to slow down and take the surroundings in. Subways and bus stations are interesting places. You'll see people sprinting from home to work and back again. You'll see students traveling to other school districts to get the best education. And you'll see a community of people who are dependent on that daily hustle.

LESS THAN ONE PERCENT

If you've ever taken the train in New York City or the light rail in San Francisco, you've inevitably seen the public transport subculture. That subculture has its own distinct infrastructure. In many ways, public transport serves as a safe haven for a city's at-risk populations. It can provide shelter from the elements or provide those who are hungry an opportunity to humbly ask for help.

Public transportation also has its own unique economy. Almost thirty million people a year pass through the Times Square Station on Forty-Second Street in New York City.[100] That traffic attracts everything from Apple personal device kiosks to homemade and somewhat unsanitary hot dog stands.

These subway subcultures also create a unique marketplace for another group of financially challenged individuals: musicians and artists. It isn't uncommon to find a guitarist, a saxophonist, or even a drummer using buckets as a makeshift percussion kit. Without a publicist or the appropriate equipment, artists share their creative canvas with millions.

Most times, those subway creatives are ignored. Other times, a commute that is otherwise sullied by the faint smell of urine is paused by sounds that don't seem to match the appearance of their composer. Rarely, there are sounds so breathtaking that many stop and stare and part with a few coins—both in acknowledgment of the musician's talent and empathy for their unfortunate plight.

January 12, 2007, wasn't one of those days. At 7:51 a.m., a man started playing a violin. Like any other day, the bustle of rush hour traffic passed him by. The violin was smooth and melodic and piercing—as string instruments can sometimes be. Cornered between

---

[100] "Market Research & Data," Transit Ridership, Times Square Official Website, accessed June 26, 2024, https://www.timessquarenyc.org/do-business/market-research-data/transit-ridership.

CHAPTER 20

the glass entry doors and the wall behind him, the artist was flanked by two yellow "wet floor" signs.

While hundreds of people engaged in their morning business, a few stopped to listen. A lady in a red coat stood a few feet away, paralyzed in awe. At one point at least five people stopped their grind and just listened. The musician took a break, and the lady in red moved on. A few other onlookers threw a few bills into his open violin case.

People came and went, but one woman kept staring and listening. The street musician stopped as if confused by her persistence. Before he could start the next song, she jumped in. "I saw you at the Library of Congress. It was fantastic! This is one of those things that could only happen in DC."[101]

He thanked her. This starving artist wasn't starving at all. This was Joshua Bell, one of the world's greatest violinists. And the violin case that morning commuters were throwing coins into wasn't just any violin case. It was a custom-built, multimillion-dollar Stradivarius. This wasn't your average rush hour commute with some insignificant artist. It was your average rush hour commute with one of the best violinists in the world, who—for a morning—was an insignificant artist.

This now famous experiment was the subject of a *Washington Post* article by Gene Weingarten.[102] Joshua Bell plays in venues that charge thousands of dollars per ticket. But on this particular day, he was a street artist. Playing to a standing ovation at the Library of Congress—

---

101 *Washington Post*, "Joshua Bell's 'Stop and Hear the Music' Metro Experiment," April 10, 2007, YouTube, https://www.youtube.com/watch?v=hnOPu0_YWhw.

102 Gene Weingarten, "Pearls before Breakfast: Can One of the Nation's Great Musicians Cut Through the Fog of a D.C. Rush Hour? Let's Find Out," *Washington Post*, April 8, 2007, https://www.washingtonpost.com/lifestyle/magazine/pearls-before-breakfast-can-one-of-the-nations-great-musicians-cut-through-the-fog-of-a-dc-rush-hour-lets-find-out/2014/09/23/8a6d46da-4331-11e4-b47c-f5889e061e5f_story.html.

something he did just recently—Joshua barely had ten people who would take a few minutes to take in the free show. This experiment highlights the challenge we have with identifying paradoxes. The environmental convention was so strong that even classical music aficionados had difficulty discerning a world-class violinist from a street musician.

Joshua's performance was no less stellar than any of his Carnegie Hall appearances. The difference was context. The venue and situation and circumstance didn't change Joshua's world-class violin-playing truth. The venue and situation and circumstance changed everyone's ability to discern that truth. It took one disruptor. It took one who didn't accept the street-music convention. It didn't matter what the context was. She knew what a world-class violinist sounded like and wouldn't let context change her ability to discern Bob Marley's truth.

Finding that truth is difficult because human beings tend to favor structure. Something that is consistently untrue is far more palatable than something inconsistently true. The fact that a famous virtuoso violinist would be playing at a subway station is a disruptive truth that's difficult to accept. It's far easier for NBA teams to play fast and shoot more three-pointers because all the other teams are doing the same thing.

That level of groupthink is comforting and predictable and free from the reflexive recoil that disruption creates. The societal and intellectual infrastructure responsible for maintaining paradoxes and fueling conventions is the same infrastructure needed to find the truth. The difference is a matter of perspective and context.

Society is a combination of truths we know, truths hidden by paradoxes and conventions, and truths yet to be discovered. Bob Marley was describing our societal construct dilemma: "Every day them get up. Them look on the TV. Them read the newspaper. Them want to see the truth, but them can't see the truth. Because the truth will not be found there."

Societal constructs cloud our ability to discern between these truths and force us into a unified perspective. If you were to see a violinist play Carnegie Hall, the venue where Joshua Bell made his debut, you'd likely assume that *anybody* playing there was a world-class musician. This desire for consistency is why tall sprinters were scuttled to other track events and why Surya Bonaly repulsed the judges.

As a society, we lack the objectivity to search for the truth without bringing our biased perspective. Unfortunately, we replace analysis with what the majority believes to be true—even when there is overwhelming evidence that what the majority believes *isn't* true. In the Joshua Bell paradox, it took one disagreeable disruptor who bravely challenged what wasn't computing in her head. She removed context from the equation and solely focused on the music—instead of the way the musician was dressed or where the musician was playing. She ignored the conventions of context, and it allowed her to see the musical truth. It's a shame she wasn't one of Surya Bonaly's judges.

Fortunately, a few people have recognized this societal deception and are actively combating this odd form of groupthink. Administrators from Toronto, Canada's largest and most diverse city, were challenged with a problem that plagues many cities around the world. Even though Toronto is well known for its uncharacteristically clean streets, the city still has challenges with graffiti. Unsightly graffiti can deface and destroy an otherwise beautiful urban landscape. In many cities, graffiti has also become a way for gangs to mark their territory.

Britannica.com defines graffiti as a "form of visual communication, usually illegal, involving the unauthorized marking of public space by an individual or group." They go on to say that "graffiti can be understood as antisocial behavior performed to gain attention or as a form of thrill-seeking," pointing out that "most jurisdictions have laws prohibiting graffiti as vandalism, and in some countries, punishment is quite severe. For example, in Singapore, violators are subject to caning. During the 1980s and 1990s, many jurisdictions sought ways to eliminate and remove graffiti, fearing that it would otherwise lead to the debasement of the community."

Most cities have teams dedicated to cleaning up and removing graffiti. Like most cities with this problem, Toronto was stuck in a graffiti quagmire. As quickly as an area was defaced, the team would swoop in to remove it. Just as quickly, that same area was defaced soon after. It was an endless cycle.

In 2012 the city of Toronto changed its tactics. Instead of focusing on graffiti removal, they focused on graffiti enhancement. Yes! They embraced graffiti. That was an uncommonly disagreeable and disruptive move. Instead of trying to change graffiti, Toronto changed the context. In a program called StreetARToronto (StART for short), city officials changed their perspective on graffiti. Instead of being the graffiti Britannica.com described—the kind of act that can even be punishable by caning—Toronto acknowledged the city's graffiti as art.

This subtle change in language marked a significant shift in perspective and context. Graffiti should be cleaned and erased. Art is cherished and revered. Most of all, art is permanent. The program also shifted the perspective of those who defaced public property. Instead of perpetrators, they became artists.

Those artists could sign up with the city and were encouraged to paint murals on public buildings. This program had the opposite effect of the *Washington Post* experiment. Instead of ignoring talented artists, Toronto put its artists on display. Anybody commissioned to use a public building as a canvas was seen as a renowned artist. That's the societal shift that occurred because of this disruptive program.

In their own words,[103]

> StreetARToronto (StART) is a suite of innovative programs designed specifically for streets and public spaces. Initiated in 2012 as an integral part of the City's Graffiti Management Plan, StART has been successful in reducing graffiti vandalism and replacing it with vibrant, colorful, community-engaged street art. StART programs make our streets more beautiful and safe, encourage active transportation (walking and cycling), showcase local artists, mentor emerging talent, and reduce overall infrastructure maintenance costs and more.

From the threat of criminal prosecution to a Michelangelo-like commission, Toronto committed to discovering its artistic version of Steph Curry. Artists who would otherwise be arrested were encouraged, mentored, and celebrated. Toronto disrupting its perspective was more effective than continuing on the same paradoxical asymptote.

When it comes to graffiti, most cities are stabilizers. They spend most of their time removing graffiti faster than other cities are removing graffiti so that they don't get relatively worse. But Toronto chose to change the context and made an effort to appreciate the work of world-class artists. They made an effort to find the truth.

---

[103] "StreetARToronto," Toronto.ca, accessed June 26, 2024, https://www.toronto.ca/services-payments/streets-parking-transportation/enhancing-our-streets-and-public-realm/streetartoronto/.

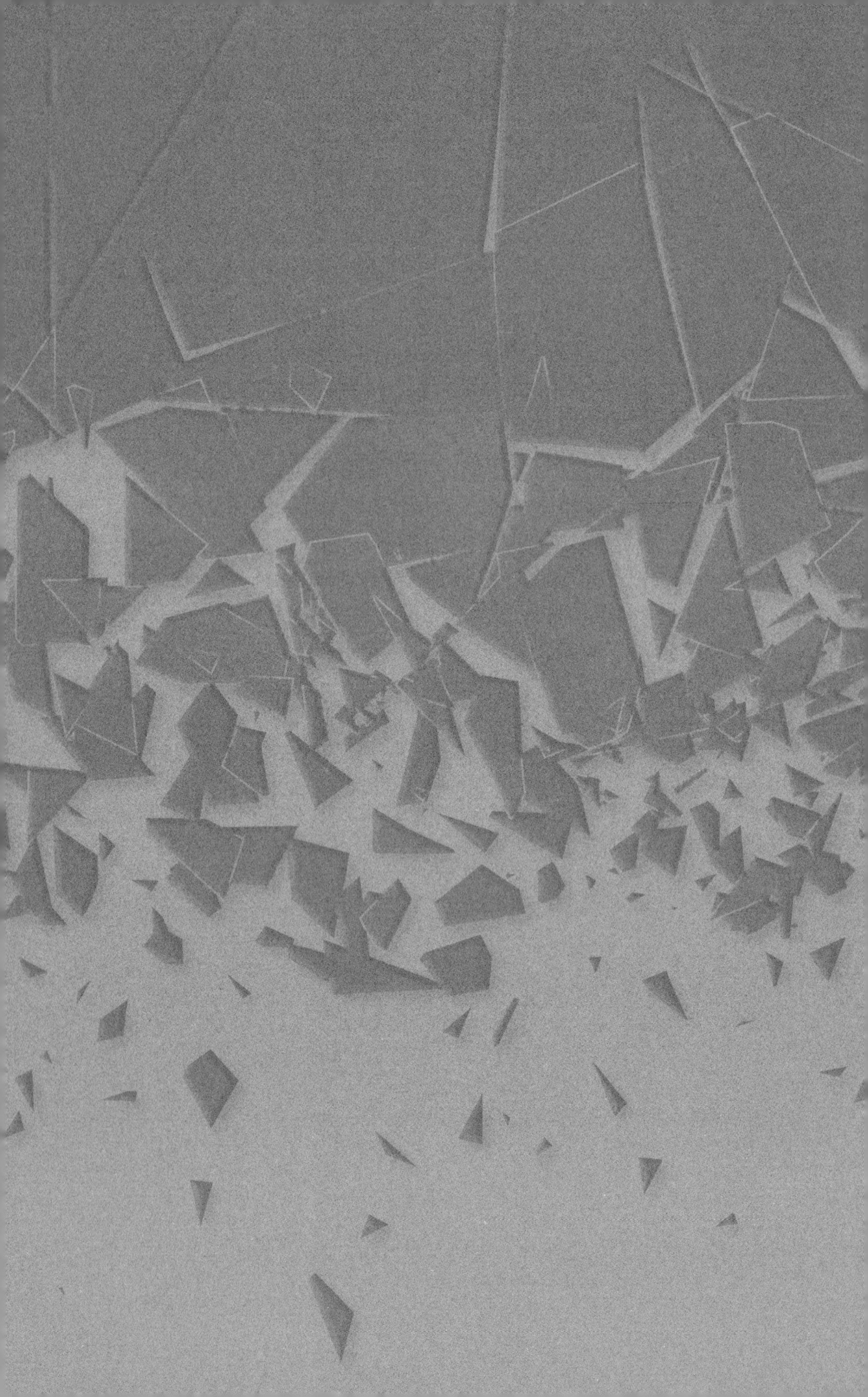

CHAPTER 21

CONSCIOUSNESS

The paradox of education is precisely this—that as one begins to become conscious one begins to examine the society in which he is being educated.

—James Baldwin

I saw him in the rearview mirror. He made a right turn and followed me. Usually, I'd pull over. But it had been a long night, and I wanted to get home.

This was the kind of morning where the mist cleared quickly as the sun changed from deep red to almost white. The drive home from a night shift is like purgatory. It's a combination of trying to wind down and unsuccessfully battling dysphoria, just as everyone else enthusiastically started their day. Every night in the emergency department is its own unique combination of Forrest Gump's box of chocolates—you never know what you're going to get. Apparently, that was the case for what should have been a routine journey home.

I hoped that the officer would just run my license plate. That's what they do most of the time. They see me, turn to follow, and then speed away after running my plate. But this one didn't. He followed so closely our cars seemed attached to each other for the entire twelve miles to my house. Two-lane roads in the morning rush are like a conveyor belt. I wanted to get away from him, but I couldn't get away from him. He was tethered to me. If I said I wasn't scared, I'd be lying. I can't remember speeding. I was glued to the speedometer and kept it just below the speed limit. I was that precise.

As I made the right turn toward my neighborhood, I was relieved the officer wasn't going to take the turn. Then he took the turn. He was back on my hip. I clicked the security gate remote and entered the neighborhood. He followed me in.

This was so confusing. I remember seeing the neighborhood waterfall. I loved how the lake reflected the sun as mist from the waterfall created miniature rainbows. But those weren't rainbows; those reflections were the red and blue lights of his police car. It was official. He was pulling me over.

I was surprised, but I wasn't surprised. I pulled out my wallet and put it on the seat before he exited his car. It always scared me to reach into my back pocket in front of the police. I looked in the rearview mirror without turning my head and started to get nervous. He was drawing his gun as he approached my car.

He asked me to put my hands outside the window, and I did. He told me to get out and lie on the ground. Slowly, I got out of the car, and he pushed me to the ground. He finally put his gun away when I was on the ground. He handcuffed me and started to pat me down.

CHAPTER 21

I lay face down on the asphalt, with my head turned to the side as neighbors drove by—rubbernecking as they passed the surreal scene. It must have looked so bizarre: a physician in hospital scrubs lying flat on the ground next to his BMW at gunpoint. There goes the neighborhood.

"Where are you going? Whose car is this?"

I answered all the officer's questions and told him that my registration was in the glove box. He went to the car's passenger side and searched the glove box. That was when he saw it, lying on the front passenger seat. He pulled out my white coat—the long white lab coat that emergency physicians wear while seeing patients—and my stethoscope. His mood changed. He asked where I worked. I told him I worked at the hospital. He picked me up, dusted me off, uncuffed me, gave me my stuff, and walked to his still-running police car. Barely audible, he mumbled, "Sorry, I thought it was stolen."

It may sound odd, but I drove home comforted. Followed for miles, pulled over, handcuffed, searched, held at gunpoint—and comforted! It wasn't an odd response because it wasn't the first time. I was comforted because, other than my pride, I was relatively unscathed.

Years earlier, as a junior in college, I faced an eerily similar situation. My roommate and I were walking home when we were confronted by an angry mob wielding bats and weapons. They were members of the hockey team, and they'd just lost the championship game. They were angry and very drunk. They surrounded us!

I charged through the wall of angry bodies they had created, while my roommate ran to our dorm. I sprinted to security and told them to call the police. I told them that the hockey team was out of control and terrorizing the campus. I begged security to call the police again. They asked me to stay with them, but I needed to make sure my roommate was all right. I found him at the front of the building, trying to hold off the mob.

Fortunately, the police showed up just in time. An officer ran up to me and asked me what had happened. As I faced him to tell him the story, I was tackled by another police officer from behind. He pressed his baton to my neck and forced his knee into the center of my back. He pulled up on the club until I couldn't breathe. I grabbed at the club but couldn't get him to stop. I couldn't even scream, and I could hear my roommate screaming at the officer. Even the hockey players were yelling at the officer. "It's not him! It's not him!" The officer kept the pressure on my neck, and I was sure I was going to die. I struggled one last time, and everything went dark.

These incidents occurred over fifteen years apart, and they were far from the only ones. After the terror, fear, and anger I felt driving home, I was overwhelmed by curiosity. I've lived in seven North American cities and was still subject to this convention. Even though I had never committed a crime, I was treated like a hardened criminal.

This police paradox has played out over and over again. It's been the subject of investigations, analysis, and a litany of well-intentioned but failed initiatives. I've played back each episode to analyze my behavior and determine if I did something to warrant the police's aggression.

These stories highlight the dangers of paradoxes and how our societal conventions can lead us astray. The officer who pulled me over performed a felony stop—a specific procedure police use to stop a vehicle suspected of harboring an individual or individuals believed to have committed a serious crime or suspects that may be armed. One reason to perform a felony stop is the suspicion of a high-end vehicle being stolen. The convention here isn't that the officer performed a felony stop. He must have believed that I was driving a stolen vehicle and that a felony stop was appropriate for that likelihood. The convention here is the reason behind the felony stop.

His words said it all: "Sorry, I thought it was stolen." The officer was ensnared in a convention, which wasn't disrupted until he found my white coat and stethoscope. That's how dangerous conventions are. These paradoxical mistakes can be harmless—but they can also have catastrophic consequences. My coach's innocent mistake in his CEO calculation comes from this inability to process data within a paradox. It comes from an inability to see through a convention to identify Bob Marley's truth. Conventions are so alluring that when they finally hit us, we can only walk away and mumble an accidental apology.

Our deference to conventions litters our society with paradoxes. Our confidence in what we believe to be true appears innocuous until we calculate the consequence of our adherence to that misrepresented status quo. In this conventional universe, Steph Curry is a one-percenter. He becomes an outlier in a world where people are shackled by conventions. Steph Curry hadn't even finished high school before he was told that 255 other basketball prospects were better than he was.

Fortunately, Bob McKillop disrupted the entire prospect evaluation system. The travesty of Stephen Curry's story isn't just the challenges that being underrated brings. The travesty of the Stephen Curry story is this question: How many other Steph Currys would there be if the approach to picking early winners and losers differed? Basketball is so great with Steph Curry, but would it have been greater with the addition of Corey Claitt or Byron Faison—if their version of Bob McKillop gave them a chance?

Inadvertently, our schools, our gyms, and our board rooms have been built for stabilizers, who rely on consensus-based rules and unscientific relationships. Predictability is far easier to pursue than truth. We prefer precision over accuracy. What do I mean? When it comes to paradoxes and conventions, we don't mind hearing that one plus one equals three—as long as one plus one always equals three. Such a calculation is precise (how repeatable a measurement or equation is) but not accurate (how close to the actual measurement or calculation is). If one plus one always equals three, that calculation is precise but obviously inaccurate.

Paradoxes and conventions work the same way. They're generated by confusing those two crucial measurement definitions. Those who can't see through paradoxes tend to see precision and accuracy as interchangeable. They also fail to recognize that accuracy can't exist in a vacuum and requires external verification and investigation. Accuracy also requires broadening our scope by attempting to analyze all possible perspectives.

My executive coach, who gave me a less-than-one-percent chance of becoming the CEO of a billion-dollar company, was looking through too narrow of a lens. He was being precise, but because of his limited scope, he wasn't accurate at all. With the scope he viewed me through then, he would likely make the same incorrect assessment all over again. One plus one would still equal three.

Like Bob Marley's truth, disruptors prefer accuracy over precision. More precisely—pun intended—they sacrifice precision in pursuit of accuracy. The correct value or measurement they're chasing is greatness. Surya Bonaly wanted to raise the bar, and that bar represented a true value. That bar represented greatness. Her competitors, mostly stabilizers, focused on precision. In other words they were decreasing the variability between performances.

Skating judges, who are also stabilizers, evaluate skaters based on their adherence to a previously submitted routine. They aren't looking for greatness. How can you submit greatness in advance? When those precision-seeking judges saw greatness in the form of a first-of-its-kind jump, they measured it as imprecise. They even failed to acknowledge the crowd's external interpretation of truth. Surya's perfectly imprecise attempt at accuracy could only be interpreted as insolence.

A more precise world, a world that aims to decrease variation, is ordinary and dull. In that world CNBC's entire disruptor list would be filled with companies trying to get better faster than the other companies were trying to get better—so that they didn't get worse. In a world based on precision, Uber would've been just another taxi company, solely focused on reducing costs to lower prices to acquire more market share. Paradoxes precisely predict outcomes of relationships that aren't accurate, and the groupthink adherence to them ignores a world teeming with greatness.

My coach believed I had less than one percent chance because of my variation. He knew that in a world of precision, I stood out. But what he failed to realize was that in a world of precision, *I stood out!* He used an arbitrary convention as the standard by which he measured my variation.

My coach's inaccurate evaluation of me is the same inaccuracy that left Surya crying beside the podium. It's the same inaccuracy that earned Stephen Curry the 256th ranking. It's the same inaccuracy that convinced the British that Nanny could never fight back and win. It's the same inaccuracy that produces students from the wealthiest country in the world who can only manage 39th best in mathematics. It's the same inaccuracy that makes city officials erase graffiti instead of embracing art. It's the same inaccuracy that only acknowledges world-class musicians in auditoriums. It's the same inaccuracy that compels parents to pay exorbitant Ivy League tuition. It's the same inaccuracy that convinces parents that parenting is about the parents. It's the same inaccuracy that convinces track coaches that sprinters should be a certain size. It's the same inaccuracy that obligates all the

NBA teams to play the same way. And it's the same inaccuracy that made an officer perform a felony stop in a lakeside community with rainbows in the background. "You feel me?" (using my best Shemar Morrow voice).

These inaccuracies continue because of our innate need for order. In the absence of external truth, these inaccuracies continue. For centuries, society has attempted to find that external truth. Science, philosophy, and religion are grounded in our truth-seeking. Like Bob Marley, it's within that truth-seeking that many of us find purpose. Those disciplines are all tools to help us investigate our accuracy—at least that's the hope.

Agreeableness keeps conventional structures intact, and it's the best way to get to groupthink. Conventions thrive without question. They thrive without the disagreeableness needed to challenge them. Like Shemar, we live in a world built for stabilizers—a world that values precision over accuracy, a world built on asymptotes devoid of truth, a world created by unfounded congruencies.

That structure forced Shemar down a road of overzealous expectation and committed him to a trajectory he was ill-equipped to maintain. The officer who pulled me over at gunpoint and the officer who choked me to near unconsciousness suffered from this same precision paradox. My car wasn't stolen, and I wasn't the one ransacking the campus. They couldn't be accurate because they were too preoccupied with precision.

These miscalculations plague a society addicted to structure and force us to compete in prescribed and predictable ways. Not only does this formula create winners and losers, but it also creates a rubric to predict winners and losers. That rubric—the calculus that we trust to make those predictions—allows human beings to reduce the entropy of life. Even when our prediction rubric is wrong, most people find comfort in its existence. In other words people would rather embrace flawed predictability than search through unpredictability to find truth. This preference lays the foundation for paradoxes, fallacies, and groupthink.

Stabilizers are particularly sensitive to this paradoxical infrastructure. Like NBA teams or parents preoccupied with their kids' Ivy League dreams, the fear of falling behind creates a societal urgency for participation. This is the fear of missing out. Even when there's no external evidence that an action will yield a desired outcome, the fear of falling behind the group keeps them in line with that group. That's why we do ridiculous things such as rank sixth-grade basketball prospects, inaccurately assess CEO potential, and give more resources to students with more resources. Some call this the rat race—our willingness to meander through an endless maze, competing without thoroughly understanding the goal.

Stabilizers unwittingly help stabilize paradoxes. They believe so devoutly in conventions that the very thought of disrupting them draws their ire. They help perpetuate the rat race—getting better faster than the others are getting better so you don't get worse. They help maintain the hustle culture. But maybe we should replace the drive to hustle harder with one to hustle differently. That's the difference between stabilizers and disruptors. That's the difference between those who need to know the rules necessary to succeed and those who see those rules as barriers to their potential greatness.

My coach was right! I was a less-than-one-percenter. I was a disruptor in a sea of stabilizers. Instead of dissuading me, he ignited my Barry O'Shea. His comment is the reason I pursued the CEO position. I almost assuredly wouldn't have pursued the job if he had calculated a far more favorable percentage. As he attempted to set the standard for a potential CEO candidate, my disagreeableness made me raise the bar.

If we consider all the challenges we have in our society, we can directly or indirectly attribute them to paradoxes. We adopt standards because we want to avoid differences. Paradoxes create an environment where a lack of diversity is more palatable than the disruption of diversity, where consistency is preferred over outliers, and where being as close to the bar as possible is preferred to raising it. It's easier to assume that graffiti brings down property values and is a sign of gang activity than it is to recognize its artistic value.

We have built our schools, our companies, and our societal infrastructure on premises that we haven't taken the time to verify. And that fact has left us with a world where our predictions have robbed us of the greatness we never knew we were missing.

CHAPTER 22

Boxes

From the moment we are born, the world tends to have a box already built for us to fit inside. Our umbilical cord never seems to be severed; we only find new needs to fill. If we disconnected and severed our attachments, would we shatter our confinements and expand beyond our shell? Would the world look different? Would we recognize ourselves? Are we the box that we are inside, and to be authentically "un-contained" would we still be able to exist? This is the irony of containment. As long as we don't push on the walls of our surroundings, we may never know how strong we really are.

—Paige Bradley

Paradoxes help give our society structure, and conventions are the scaffolding in that paradoxical edifice. According to *Cambridge Dictionary,* society is "a large group of people who live together in an organized way, making decisions about how to do things and sharing the work that needs to be done." Don't get me wrong, rules are necessary, but often, what we believe are rules aren't rules at all. Nanny and the Maroons lived in a world where rules subjugated them to a life of oppression. Even though those rules were immoral and unjust, they were part of Jamaica's social framework.

Disruption separates rules from conventions. It's the mechanism by which the truth can be assessed. The disagreeableness that disruptors use to shatter conventions isn't from a disdain for rules. This disagreeableness that disruptors use to shatter conventions is from a disdain for rules that shouldn't be rules at all. That's the truth that Marley was talking about. And it's the box that Paige Bradley wrote about.

The police officer who pulled me over at gunpoint followed me for twenty-one miles. If we include the stoplights along the way, that's about thirty minutes. For thirty minutes, the officer followed closely behind me! What was he doing for thirty minutes?

Police officers are trained to analyze situations to determine the likelihood of a potential crime. Profiling is a way to evaluate individuals based on specific criteria. In other words it's a way to put potential criminals in a box. For example, police look for signs that a driver might be driving under the influence. Officers are taught to look for the following: a flushed appearance, an alcohol smell on the breath, fumbling with one's wallet when asked for identification, not comprehending an officer's requests or questions, lack of coordination or balance when standing, being defensive or combative, disheveled appearance, and not knowing the time or location. Alone, any of these criteria might not be cause for alarm. But in combination, they're highly predictive of someone who is a danger to other drivers on the road.

It took thirty minutes to determine whether a physician driving home at the crack of dawn fit into a box. After half an hour of assessing and analyzing, he determined that the BMW I was driving must have been stolen. Based on his criteria and the conventions he applied to create them, he had a strong reason to believe that my BMW contained a driver or passenger suspected of having committed a serious crime, especially of a nature that would lead him to believe that I may be armed.

The officer put me in the felony stop box. His mind couldn't fathom that I was simply a physician driving home after caring for patients in the emergency department—an emergency department within his jurisdiction. He was looking for precision (how close the situation resembled the criteria for a felony stop) instead of accuracy (a physician driving home in a BMW after a long night shift).

When he found my stethoscope and physician lab coat, his quest for precision was shattered by accuracy. How did he get it so wrong? What made his calculation a miscalculation? To find that answer, let's examine how paradoxes manifest themselves and how stabilizers sometimes build an inaccurate reality around them.

Part of a police officer's duty is to uphold the law. Although they sometimes require interpretation, laws serve as society's rules. If someone is apprehended for breaking the law, there isn't much room to debate the law itself. Through the legal process, an individual can argue how closely they followed the rule. But the law itself still stands. In this way the law becomes a standard, and the determination of guilt or innocence is based on how closely one adheres to this asymptote.

As stabilizers, police work functionally toward asymptotes. Their success is determined by how closely they adhere to the laws that they enforce. To do so, they knowingly or unknowingly force individuals and situations into constructs that fit. Police officers' greatest strength is their precision, which may also be their greatest weakness.

Bob Marley and Surya Bonaly aren't only disruptors; they're creatives. Writers, photographers, videographers, musicians, artists, and actors are all members of this exclusive club. These individuals use imagination and inspiration to create new things from scratch. Being an excellent creative requires thinking outside the box. It requires an understanding of the rules, an acceptance of those rules, and then an ability to reject some components of those rules to deliver a creative outcome.

Marley followed some of reggae's conventions, but he rejected many others. The music industry had never seen an artist like Marley before. His unique sound was only part of his creative disruption. His true creativity was his disagreeable approach to his message. That kind of creativity is a hallmark of disruptors, and it presents a unique challenge to stabilizers, especially police.

The late rapper Nipsey Hussle described the creative challenge for stabilizers in a 2009 interview.[104]

> What I know about life is that you gon hurt yourself, you know ... especially as a creative. Creativity and competition is opposites, you know what I'm saying ... They were against each other. Creatively, you have to draw from a blank canvas. You got to draw from your pool of experiences for it to have that thing in it. And you can compete and make something that's like technically good.... That's a different formula. So I think that to create is like a natural labor. And then to copy or to like compare or compete, creatively, you confuse yourself.

Nipsey didn't just illuminate the conundrum between stabilizers and disruptors. He also highlighted the police officer's dilemma. Competition is an asymptote. It's a never-ending process of getting

---

104 djvlad, "Nipsey Hussle on Spirituality, Telling the Truth, Creating Timeless Music (Full Interview)," April 1, 2020, YouTube, https://www.youtube.com/watch?v=qH1YGFls1RQ.

better faster than others are getting better so you don't get worse. Police officers don't want to get worse! If a police officer fails, the results could be catastrophic.

The officer followed me for thirty minutes because he was conflicted in his creativity. Stabilizers need boxes, and when I didn't fit into any of those boxes, he couldn't bear to use his creativity to find a different answer. So he forced me into the stolen-BMW-felony-stop box instead of using his creativity to find a more disruptive answer.

That is the lesson of Usain Bolt, Steph Curry, Nanny, Surya Bonaly, and Bob Marley. Society has a way of creating boxes for us all to fit into. Sometimes, we're forced into a box we don't want to be in. But more often than not, we inadvertently force ourselves into boxes we never ever wanted to be in.

Where we fall down is in the idea that being a disruptor is something unique or that being disagreeable is something that requires a particular disposition. The truth is that disruption is as easy as rejecting our boxes and replacing competition with creativity without confusing ourselves.

How might the world change if we shatter our confinements and cut our umbilical cords? That's the real resistance to greatness: the fear of not even recognizing what we are or what we could be if we—just for a moment—step out of our box. If we stop being so precise and set off in search of actuals, greatness is no longer only for outliers. Disruption isn't reserved for a few. It's the ability to be authentically uncontained. Stabilizers focus on maintaining the box and avoid pushing on the walls. Surya, Bob, and Nanny made the leap and found out how strong they really were by disconnecting from their attachments. Disruption isn't about disrupting things. It's about disrupting oneself.

Marley describes that very box.[105]

---

105 metisrastaman, "Bob Marley Interview 1979."

> There's a force fighting against, not just the music but the truth. Yeah, because sometime the truth is like a two-edged sword. You know, it cut sharp. That mean plenty people don't like hear the truth. Because plenty people find themselves feeling guilty. So the truth is an offense.

Bob and Paige were describing the same thing. Bob referred to those tethers that bind us in terms of the television and the newspaper: "Every day them get up. Them look on the TV. Them read the newspaper. Because the truth will not be found there." The box that limits our authentically uncontained selves will never be shattered unless we cut the umbilical cord that streams conventions into our souls.

"Them want to see the truth, but them can't see the truth. Because the truth will not be found there." If we all took the time to break out from the chains of our agreeableness, imagine how different the world would be. Without the confinements we've artificially created, how much more greatness would exist in our world? How much more truth would we be able to attain? How many more world-class basketball players, virtuoso violinists, record-breaking sprinters, freedom fighters, hall-of-fame figure skaters, and multibillion-dollar CEOs would there be?

If we could challenge these paradoxical constructs that limit us, not only would we be better as individuals, but our entire society would also be better. Instead of a society preoccupied with getting better faster than everybody else is getting better so they don't get worse, we could build a society focused on raising the bar.

This is the challenge of paradox and convention. We perceive our roles in this universe dichotomously. We believe we're either one or the other: winners or losers, stabilizers or disruptors, CEOs or non-CEOs. Paradoxes don't exist in the world. They exist within

CHAPTER 22

each and every one of us. Disruption doesn't describe the relationship between an individual and the rest of the world. Disruption describes the relationship between an individual and themselves.

From our first day of kindergarten to yesterday in the office, we're taught to agreeably remain tethered because we're worried the world may look different. We're worried that we won't recognize ourselves. To find out how strong we really are, we must risk our very existence. That's the heart of disruption, to risk one's existence in the pursuit of greatness.

To land that backflip, we have to risk falling. We have to risk drawing the ire of the judges. We have to risk the wrath of the entire British army. And yes, the chances of greatness outside the box are far less than the chances of mediocrity inside it. That calculation is one that each of us has to make while immersed in the quagmire of conventions.

We often misunderstand those calculations. I misunderstood those calculations. I thought "less than one percent" described my chances of becoming the CEO. I thought it described my coach's assessment of my ability and merit. I viewed his comment as a stabilizer, an individual trapped in a box filled with asymptotes. I was in the rat race. My coach's comment was an assessment, but it was also much more than that. His comment was directional.

Less than one percent was instructive and allowed me to channel my inner Barry O'Shea. Less than one percent described the role I had to play in the world. Stabilizers focus on the 99 percent—most of what is agreeable and inside that box. Disruptors, though, live in a disconnected world of bar raising and box shattering—a world reserved for the less than one percent.

207

> *General impressions are never to be trusted. Unfortunately when they are of long standing they become fixed rules of life, and assume a prescriptive right not to be questioned. Consequently, those who are not accustomed to original inquiry entertain a hatred and a horror of statistics. They cannot endure the idea of submitting their sacred impressions to cold-blooded verification. But it is the triumph of scientific men [and women] to rise superior to such superstitions, to devise tests by which the value of beliefs may be ascertained, and to feel sufficiently masters of themselves to discard contemptuously whatever may be found untrue.*
>
> –Francis Galton

DENOUEMENT

SPIRITUAL LEADER

The truth is like a lion; you don't have to defend it. Let it loose; it will defend itself.

–Saint Augustine

Becoming the CEO of a multibillion-dollar organization may have been a surprise to my professional coach. But if he paid closer attention, it wouldn't have been much of a surprise at all—not because of skills or experience or politics but because of something far less obvious.

It was no small accident that the son of Michael and Pauline reacted to that perceived slight the way I did. Michael Tomlinson and Pauline Chambers chose the name Imamu Osei—Swahili for "spiritual leader"—because they knew something that my professional coach didn't.

My parents are both from the "wi likkle but wi tallawah" island of Jamaica. And like most Jamaican descendants, they had inherited and passed on Nanny's disagreeableness, optimism, and relentlessness.

Pauline, a chartered accountant, and Michael, a serial entrepreneur, passed on Bob Marley's compulsion with the truth.

With an indomitable cultural heritage like that, I had no choice. I had to disrupt that CEO paradox. My professional coach's assessment of how I fit into the status quo was necessary to Barry-O'Shea me into something I never knew I wanted.

I am a child of two immigrants who became an immigrant myself. In all that cultural upheaval, I remained inexorably tied to the culture that raised me. And it isn't just Nanny and Marley and Bolt. The makeup of my CEO persona was crafted and cultivated in the heart of a country 1,755 miles from where I was born.

That cultural essence found its way to frigid Canada, shuttled in the dreams of two Jamaicans who independently migrated to a new world—a world filled with promise but reluctant to accept them. However, that lineage wasn't reserved for just my parents. My mother's mother was an elementary school teacher who shaped the heart and minds of early Jamaicans. My father's mother, a seamstress, made dresses for the family business—a job made even more challenging by the fact that she had lost her vision from an aggressive form of glaucoma.

That lineage of disagreeableness was even more evident on one of my many visits to Jamaica. Walking through a prison is the kind of thing that would shock any preadolescent child. And walking through a prison in a borderline third-world country is that much more shocking. Some yelled for help, and others pleaded and vehemently argued their innocence, but most of them shouted vile, threatening (and uniquely Jamaican) epithets as we walked.

That's when a tall prisoner at the back of one of the cells roared up to the bars and yelled in a deep and grizzly voice, "Boss, when you a go let me out a dis place?"

DENOUEMENT

I jumped back. The prisoner looked strong enough to topple the rusting cage that held him. I didn't know whether to stop walking or run. I felt a hand on my shoulder and heard a comforting voice. "Bwoy, stop you foolishness. You scaring the child."

The "Boss" the prisoner was referring to was my aunt, Jasmine Tomlinson-Brown—or Auntie Jas, as we called her. She was the first female police superintendent in Western Jamaica, and she was in charge.[106] She walked through this prison full of male inmates and male officers and had everyone under her control.

In a world that often didn't treat her with the respect she deserved, she served with grace and civility. She even respected those who chose not to respect her, including the prisoners who tried their utmost to unnerve her.

To be the first female leader in a male-dominated discipline, whose purpose is to police mostly male criminals, requires the disagreeableness of a disruptor. I'm not sure if she had a coach who gave her the same dismal odds that I would receive years later, but she definitely had her detractors. I struggled to carry the weight of her story in a church that was far too small for all those there to honor her. She passed away in 2022.

The cultural consistency of my lineage is now abundantly clear. Nanny, Marley, Usain, my grandparents, my parents, and Auntie Jas all spent a lifetime disrupting the status quo. Disagreeableness isn't exclusively Jamaican, but it is absolutely intrinsic to Jamaica. That disruptive lineage made its way to me. I, in turn, passed it on to my children.

---

106 "History-Making Former Policewoman Jasmine Tomlinson-Brown Dies," *Gleaner*, August 9, 2022, https://jamaica-gleaner.com/article/news/20220809/history-making-former-policewoman-jasmine-tomlinson-brown-dies.

My son—better known to my daughter as "Bubby"—remained seizure-free, went on to play college basketball, and is on the dean's list. He disrupted the seizure paradox.

My daughter—who is five foot five on a good day—was ranked by ESPN as one of the top one hundred high school female basketball players in the country (and you know how I feel about rankings). She disrupted the only-tall-players-can-succeed-at-basketball paradox. Like another Jamaican, Fraser-Price, my daughter succeeded because of her stature and not in spite of it.

Less than One Percent isn't a search for the thing that separates winners and losers; it's a search for those who win even when they have no business doing so. It highlights a world guilty of not only obscuring the truth but also of normalizing the idea that we've already found it. And disruption? Disruption is the tool necessary to tease out the signal from the noise. Disruption is the lens that allows us to see through the social structures that only exist to support our dependency on them.

For me, the world is full of paradoxes in need of disruption, partially—or maybe more than partially—because of who I was compelled to be. Disruption is intrinsic to who I am, but it isn't an exclusive club. Hopefully, *Less than One Percent* has made a reasonable argument that the world would be a better place if we *all* were inspired to use our unique combination of gifts to impact the world. Our individual ability to succeed isn't dependent on some conventional—and in many cases arbitrary—standard.

And even more, we have a responsibility to play our part to create a world where anybody—no matter what unique skills and shortcomings they have—can be greater than anyone believed they could be. That is the truth we should continue to seek each and every day of our lives. That is the truth sought out by the less than one percent.

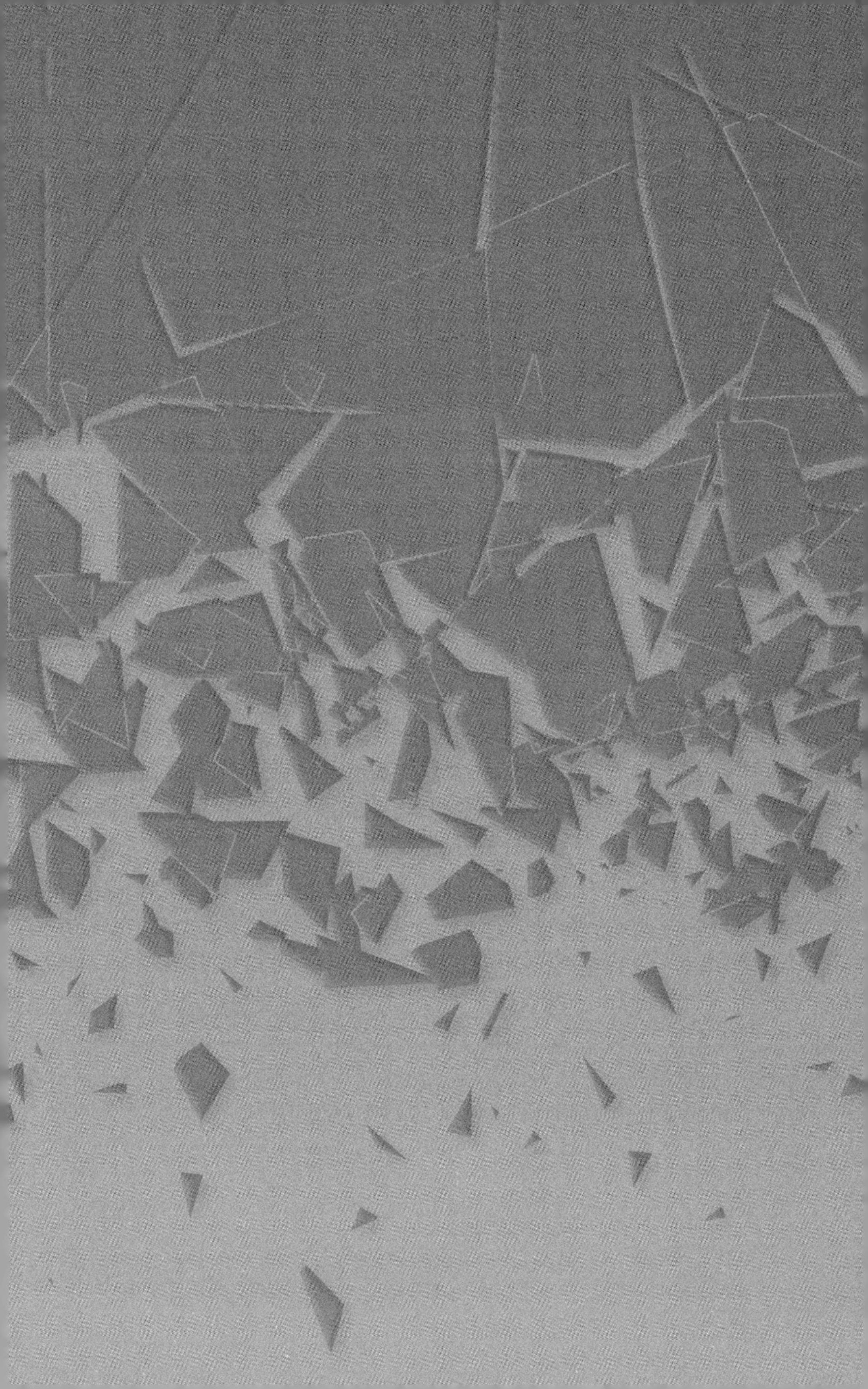

ALMOST...